Garth Brooks has pu... ...r as they'll go. Unwilling to play it safe by Nashville standards, he made a powerful and provocative video of his song "The Thunder Rolls," which depicted an abusive husband's violent end. The video was banned by the Nashville Network and Country Music Television—and then won Music Video of the Year at the Country Music Association Awards. His number one album, *Ropin' the Wind*, features a powerhouse pop-inspired cover of Billy Joel's "Shameless," a move Garth himself calls a major artistic risk. His dynamic stage presence, his fierce loyalty to his fans, and his contagious enthusiasm have helped Garth Brooks capture the hearts of millions!

WINNER OF FOUR 1991 COUNTRY MUSIC ASSOCIATION AWARDS

- Single of the Year, for "Friends in Low Places"
- Album of the Year, for *No Fences*
- Music Video, "The Thunder Rolls"
                    and
- **Entertainer of the Year**

GARTH BROOKS

☆

A BIOGRAPHY

Michael McCall

BANTAM BOOKS
NEW YORK • TORONTO • LONDON • SYDNEY • AUCKLAND

GARTH BROOKS

A Bantam Book / December 1991

Packaged by March Tenth, Inc.
Designed by Stanley S. Drate, Folio Graphics Co., Inc.

ISBN 0-553-29823-2

Published simultaneously in the United States and Canada

Bantam Books are published by Bantam Books, a division of
Bantam Doubleday Dell Publishing Group, Inc. Its trademark,
consisting of the words, "Bantam Books" and the portrayal of a
rooster, is Registered in U.S. Patent and Trademark Office and in
other countries. Marca Registrada. Bantam Books, 666 Fifth
Avenue, New York, New York 10103.

PRINTED IN THE UNITED STATES OF AMERICA

RAD   0 9 8 7 6 5 4 3

Chapter

☆ 1 ☆

On September 23, 1991, Garth Brooks made American music history. On that day, the burly twenty-nine-year-old singer from Oklahoma became the first country singer to put out an album and see it leap to the number-one spot on the national pop charts the week of its release. "It's a historic accomplishment," declared the associate director of retail research at *Billboard* magazine. "As best as we can determine, it's the first time it's happened."

The first, that is, for a country music artist.

In the month prior to the album's release, record retailers sent more than two million orders (another country music first) for Garth's *Ropin' the Wind* to Capitol Records. As retail executives wisely had anticipated, fans across

America hurriedly pushed through the doors of record stores to purchase Garth's newest recording on the first day it was put on sale.

In Houston, a store manager reported that fans stood four-thick in a line snaking across more than three city blocks, as people from ages fifteen to fifty excitedly yet patiently waited for their chance to lasso a copy of their own. Many bought two, three, four copies or more, hauling the extra cassettes and compact discs to friends and family members so they, too, could immediately hear the complete collection without having to endure a similar queue.

The unprecedented buying frenzy didn't just occur in the South and Southwest, where Garth's name and image rate on a recognition level once reserved for pop music icons Bruce Springsteen, Madonna, and Michael Jackson. In Sacramento, a retail record store manager reported that more than three hundred people swarmed into the parking lot prior to the 10 A.M. opening. Nearly a thousand more record buyers carried the new Garth Brooks collection through the check-out line before the store closed late that night.

The album even sold well in areas without country music radio stations. In Cambridge, Massachusetts, Harvard students swept through stores to hook an early copy. In Mankato, Minnesota, home of Mankato State University, a store clerk reported "great" sales to *Billboard* magazine, saying students had become familiar with Garth's music by hearing it in bars and at parties. In Lincoln, Nebraska, prime Garth country, a store near the University of Nebraska had sold out of CDs and cassettes by 3 P.M. the first day they were put in the racks.

In Nashville, the executive responsible for making sure his retail record chain remains stocked with popular titles exclaimed, "What's the expression? 'It's blowing out the roof!'"

The plants used by Capitol Records to spin music onto cassette tape and encode it digitally onto compact discs had been working overtime for weeks to try to fill the advance orders pouring in for the new album. Workers stayed on the job through Labor Day weekend and every weekend through September to keep up with the overwhelming and unexpected demand. The first two million copies flew out of stores almost as fast as they were unpacked. The first week's total topped 2.6 million. By then, Capitol had received requests for more than another million. The Capitol plants kept rolling and packing and trucking, rolling and packing and trucking, rolling and packing and trucking.

* * *

On September 23, the day Garth's album first sat atop the world of pop, an overcast sky dropped a soft, cleansing rain on Nashville, Tennessee, as if the skies were ceremoniously washing away the years of second-class citizenship that country music has endured for more than three decades. The music created in Nashville had long been relegated to the same status as jazz, big band music, and popular vocalists like Rosemary Clooney—an audience still existed for the music, but it no longer drew the masses it had in the past.

By the afternoon, the sun was shining brightly on Nashville, and a crisp, refreshing breeze blew down the streets where country music is written, played, and recorded. The success of this young upstart named Garth Brooks presented the hope of a new dawn for country music. His ability to reach new audiences generated an intoxicating enthusiasm through Nashville's music industry. The electricity of unbridled expectation crackled in the executive suites, the recording studios, and on the street. The Nashville record business was stepping with a newfound confidence and optimism. For the first time since Hank Williams had died and Elvis Presley had swiveled his hips, a man who proudly declared himself a country music artist ranked as the most popular male performer in the United States.

Music fans who fought acne and carried algebra books were buying his tapes without having to hide them from peers; broad-shouldered football players shouted through the din at fraternity parties to request that his songs be blared through the speakers, and their suggestions were met by cheers of approval instead of jeers of disgust.

Few country performers who create their music in Nashville have experienced success beyond the traditional country audience. By the 1970s, country's core audience crossed most cultural and educational lines, but its backbone remained that of working-class Southerners and their relatives who had migrated to urban industrial areas across America.

Every once in a blue moon, an iconoclastic performer has broken outside the country formula and caught the ear of a wider audience: Roger Miller did it by snapping his fingers with beat-poet cool while singing about life as a wayward hitchhiker in "King of the Road," a song that catapulted Miller to a sweep of the 1965 Grammy Awards. Johnny Cash's imposing figure cut through the heartland when his earnest, brooding populism was featured on network television and struck a chord with the counterculture as well as mainstream America for a period in the late 1960s. And before that, Marty Robbins had reached the letter sweater set with the prom-ready "A White Sport Coat (And a Pink Carnation)," the soft-bopping "Singing the Blues," and the Spanish-tinted western drama of "El Paso." But those examples of success had faded quickly, and Nashville went back to trying to keep the small audience it already held.

But the promise of lodging a star at the pinnacle of music popularity began fading for Nashville performers at about the same time Elvis Presley first curled his lip at a television camera. Despite the odd breakthrough, Nashville and country music never regained stature in the cultural pantheon dominated by the taste of young America. Country music attracted a loyal, core audience, and most performers were satisfied with repaying that loyalty by staying inside self-imposed limits.

Garth Brooks has broken those barriers, with only the slightest hint of calculated effort. Like Roy Acuff and Hank Williams, he's unafraid to reveal deep emotions in his songs and performances. He has weeped when accepting honors and awards, while fighting the tears and cursing his weakness. His music covers the profane and the sacred, and he becomes physically and emotionally animated performing his best songs. Whether performing the rowdy, Everyman anthem "Friends in Low Places" or the fragile, spiritually philosophical "The Dance," he appears to connect completely with the message and to communicate the intensity of his feelings to an audience.

Hank Williams once described the secret of a good country music performance by saying, "It can be explained in just one word: *sincerity*. When a hillbilly sings a crazy song, he feels crazy. When he sings 'I Laid My Mother Away,' he sees her a-laying right there in the coffin."

When Garth rushes to the lip of a stage to shout, "I'm shameless," he's describing that same instinctual craziness Hank described. When he wipes a tear while singing "If Tomorrow Never Comes," he's showing the tangle of emotions he still feels when he thinks of a college friend who died young. He connects on an unusually deep level with the content of his songs, he'll tell anyone who will listen. He communicates those feelings in an intimate, subtly dramatic way that his audience responds to. He establishes the kind of connection that draws people to line up outside of a store to hear what's next.

Chapter

☆ 2 ☆

Garth became the sixth and last child to join the Brooks clan, born Troyal Garth Brooks on February 7, 1962. By then the Brooks family closely resembled a typical middle-class Oklahoma family. His father, Troyal Raymond Brooks, was firm, stoic, and strict yet loving and supportive. His mother, Colleen Carroll Brooks, had been a featured singer on a weekly TV show before settling down.

Recently, Garth would describe his mother affectionately as "a nut," and go on at length about her goofy sense of humor and playful nature. She desires attention, something both she and her son admit. She likes flashy clothes and glittery accessories. Since her son's rise to stardom, her fashion sense has grown more outrageous, tending toward loud colors and fancy embellishments. She likes to have her nails decorated with sparkling beads, and she attended a recent country music banquet in a long dress completely covered in flashing, multicolored sequins. She's also got a naturally effervescent personality, finding a positive slant in nearly everything. She bubbles with joy daily, her son says. She also cries easily, openly, and often, wearing her emotions on the surface. That's another trait she passed on to her son.

Ray is as low-key and stolid as his wife is lively and outgoing. However, he could vent rage when his children stepped out of line, and he intimidated the family with imposing strictness. He laid the law down, Garth has said, and it was not to be broken without consequences. He can be very stubborn. But, beneath his bullheaded exterior is a big heart and a loving man.

"If I could wrap my dad up in two words, it would be 'thundering tenderness,'" Garth has said. "He's a man with the shortest temper I ever saw, and at the same time he's got the biggest heart. Some of the greatest conflicts are not between two people but between one person and himself. He knows what's right and he doesn't have any tolerance for what isn't right, but at the same time he is so forgiving. I learned from him that you gotta be thankful for what you got and treat people like you want to be treated. My dad drilled that into my head all my life. We're a lot alike in that way."

The whole family remains close to this day, say the parents and the children. Though the six children actually have three sets of parents among them (both Ray and Colleen were married before), they don't tolerate any suggestions that there is any lack of loyalty or love between them. As for the term half-brother or half-sister, Garth has said, "We don't believe in the term. There were a lot of fights in town because of that term."

Garth's sister, Betsy Smittle, is the other musical member of the family. She joined Garth's band in 1990, becoming the only replacement since her brother formed his band, Stillwater, in 1988. Kelly, the only child besides Garth to share Ray and Colleen as biological parents, works with Garth as his tour accountant. The two also roomed in college and refer to each as best friends. Garth, when asked who he's closest to in the world, points to Kelly instead of his wife Sandy, his parents, or any other friend. "My family is still my biggest influence," Garth has said.

His mother confirms that bonds remain tight between Garth and all of his siblings. "He is a family-oriented person," Colleen Brooks noted. "I raised my family to love God, their family, and their country, in that order. Garth follows that to this day, and I'm very proud of the way he's turned out. He knows what's real, and it gives him an anchor. That's why I'm not afraid of how he's going to deal with all this attention. He's good, solid people."

As Colleen suggests, Ray and Colleen Brooks reared their children on values that Garth openly continues to promote today. As his mother proudly boasts, "Garth says he wants to bring prayer back to the dinner table and an American flag to the front porch."

The rest of the family followed suit: There were no Vietnam War protesters in the family, no high school dropouts, no one who is known or even thought to have a problem with drugs.

Despite their son's appearances in clubs, Ray and Colleen Brooks don't really go for nightlife. Yukon doesn't offer much beyond the local veteran's club, and the couple doesn't go into Oklahoma City often. They prefer family get-togethers. They have always taken their children to Baptist church regularly on Sunday, participated in church socials, and followed the boys to sporting events.

But they both love music. The couple's taste are similar, leaning toward a gritty, honest, emotion-drenched style of country music known as honky-tonk. Hank Williams, Sr., and George Jones were early favorites in their courtship, and their affection for the music of the two country music legends remains firm today.

Raymond and Colleen understood the lifestyle and the emotional battles that their heroes put into music. But they were able to work through whatever troubles and temptations arose in their lives. They held themselves and their family together through a period of American history that saw the generation gap expand greatly and ultimately tore many families apart.

Raymond and Colleen had other favorites, such as Merle Haggard and Marty Robbins. The couple were buying and playing Haggard's records, for instance, long before he commemorated their state, their belief system, and their way of life in his song "Okie From Muskogee."

But "Okie From Muskogee" only made the couple appreciate Haggard all the more. The song was released in 1969, a year after the Democratic Convention in Chicago revealed to the rest of the country violent differences between the country's leadership and a youth movement rebelling against what it considered America's political and social inequities, which had been brought to a head by the Vietnam War. It came much closer to capturing the allegiances of the Brooks family than, say, the songs "Revolution" by the Beatles or "Street Fightin' Man" by the Rolling Stones. Haggard sang of being proud to be an Okie from Muskogee, "a place where even squares can have a ball."

Before long, Garth was singing the words along with his parents in the backyard of their home. "We had music around the house twenty-four hours a day, it seemed," Garth recalled. He doesn't suggest he purposefully emulated or overtly enjoyed listening to these songs of adult concerns while in elementary school. But it was there, and he didn't mind it, either. "When I look back, I was soaking in it quite a bit," he said. Decades later, his incubation period would return to exert an influence on his musical tastes that he wasn't aware of initially.

His mother also continued to perform, if only for the children on weekend cookouts. She would pull out her guitar and everyone—Dad, all six kids—joined in singing and dancing and carrying on. Betsy was the first to take up music seriously; she can now play anything with strings or keys. "She's one of the best instrumentalists around," her youngest brother and current boss says.

Garth was an enthusiastic participant in

these gatherings. His mother bought him a banjo when he was young. Garth fooled around with it, but he was too caught up in hanging out with his friends and playing every sport that came along to devote much time to practicing the intricate exercises needed to learn to make chords on a banjo.

Later, though, he taught himself to play an acoustic guitar, which he learned with much more focus and ease than the banjo. As for his singing ability, his mother can recall giving him breath control lessons and instructing him in how to enunciate words for greater dramatic effect. But Garth was usually off experimenting on his own. He wasn't patient enough for lessons, his mother said. She figures it hasn't hurt him much, she'll add with a smile.

Chapter

☆ 3 ☆

Garth Brooks may be soft-spoken now, but it's a trait acquired in adulthood. To hear his family tell of it, the Brooks family has always been loud. And Garth was not only the youngest, but the loudest.

His family remembers him as a rambunctious, funny youngster who loved to be the center of attention and often proved entertaining once he grabbed the spotlight.

In interviews he tells a slightly different story. He believes he was a dreamer with grand ideas of what he would become as an adult. He wanted to be a baseball player, often dreaming of smacking long home runs, diving to snag difficult catches, and always winning the big games.

Sometimes he dreamed of entertaining people, but he just as likely would be an actor in a movie as a singer on a stage. At other times he dreamed of working as a forest ranger, working amid tall oaks, sprawling lakes, and wild animals. He saw himself as a romantic ranger who politely assisted people in the ways of the wilds while occasionally stomping out fires, rescuing stranded campers, or nursing injured bears.

Yukon, as Garth puts it, "is an average city in the middle of average Oklahoma in the middle of average America." The town provides the basics of what most small-town families and farming communities need: A few gas stations, several grocery stores, a Wal-Mart, proximity to a mall.

His family still tells stories of what once was known as "Funny Night" at the Brooks household, when everyone would stand up and act foolish. They might act out skits from television shows and try to create long, rambling, hilarious tales that became more grandiose as they went on. Garth nearly always stole the show one way or another.

By the time he reached high school, he was among the more popular youngsters in Yukon. He was a handsome, broad-shouldered teenager with hair nearly down to his shoulders which he kept well-groomed. He dressed like most student athletes, wearing jeans, T-shirts, and sweaters, occasionally showing up in sweat pants. He wore sneakers instead of boots. If he had on a hat, it would be a baseball cap, not a ten-gallon cowboy hat.

As a star athlete, he ran with the in-crowd. He played quarterback and tight end on the football team, guiding it through the beginning of the season as offensive leader. That the team lost its first five games was of little consequence on campus; Garth was quarterback, and there was no position more cherished by his peers. He also was a decent baseball pitcher and outfielder who liked swinging for the fences. In track and field he ran the middle distances and messed around with pole vaulting, the discus, and the shot put.

But Garth not only was a favorite among the most popular students on campus. He befriended teachers and classroom aides, and he went out of his way to make small talk with the shy students who didn't fit in with the cooler crowd.

"Garth was definitely in the in-crowd," recalled Tim Campbell, a fellow student who now lives in Piedmont, Oklahoma. "Everyone liked him. You know, he went out with the best-looking girls, played all of the sports, all of that. And I wasn't in that crowd at all. I was shy and didn't really fit in well back then.

"But the thing I remember about Garth was that he went out of his way to talk to me and be nice to me. We weren't friends or anything like that. But where a lot of the guys he ran around with would kind of bully people like me, Garth wasn't like that at all. He was genuinely a nice guy, and nearly everyone else in that crowd wouldn't give me the time of day."

Campbell did participate in track as a runner, but he wasn't among the better athletes. He recalls Garth sidling up to him to offer encouragement and tips. "He once told me to eat honey before a meet, that it would help give me more energy," Tim recalled. "I just remember him as a nice guy, real personable and real talkative. He was definitely popular. I think everybody would have remembered him even if he wasn't famous now. He just had that kind of personality. He was everybody's friend."

Larry Lo Baugh was Garth's football coach in high school. Now principal of Yukon High, Lo Baugh is a mild-mannered, polite man who is well-liked by his students and faculty. He also recalls Garth as a friendly, personable young fellow who was active at school. He wasn't exactly a model student; his grades were slightly above average. But, as Lo Baugh put it,

"He was a fine young man with a lot of character."

As a football player, Garth was a gung-ho leader. "He was a fierce competitor," Lo Baugh remembered with affection. "He started at tight end, then was moved to quarterback his senior year. He was a good player. . . . [A] leader. He was very open, and he didn't mind expressing his opinion. He'd really encourage the other players, and pat them on the back when they did something good. And he didn't mind getting on them a little."

He also remembers something unusual about Garth: He was a jock who liked to read. "I know he liked English, which certainly wasn't the norm for a football player," Lo Baugh laughed. "He liked being on stage, too, acting out a lot. He was a real joker. But when it came to getting serious, he was right there in front. He was very well liked. He had a big circle of friends."

Veda Eby, who works in the principal's office at Yukon High, points out that Garth used to drop by just to say hello and chat with the office workers. "He was real sincere, a friendly guy," she recalled about Yukon's most famous graduate. "We sure didn't have any idea he would turn out to be a singer like he has. He played sports here, and that's pretty much how he was known. We're real proud of him here."

Eby describes the Brooks family as well-behaved and active, suggesting Troy and Colleen raised a bunch of good kids who enjoyed themselves and made others feel good.

"He came from a good family, all of his brothers and sisters were popular and were good students," says the longtime Yukon High employee. "It's just hard to believe what all's happened to him. You never think of one of the students going on to be a famous entertainer, I guess."

Patsy Woods, a Yukon High English instructor, also remembers Garth with fondness. She taught him in a ninth-grade "honors English class," a special class for those who have shown an exceptional aptitude for reading and writing at their grade level.

"I remember Garth as a really good person, a big, warm-hearted kind of guy," Woods said. "Mostly, I remember the fact that he was a good student and had a good personality. A lot of students are shy at that age, but Garth was very personable, very comfortable with himself."

He enjoyed reading, and talked eloquently about philosophy and ideas in class. His teacher laughed at one incident in particular:

"We were reading Shakespeare's *Romeo and Juliet*, and Garth was reading Romeo's part," his instructor noted. "We weren't acting it out. He was just supposed to read it. But Garth would read it real dramatically. He would act out even though it wasn't necessary. He just enjoyed it. When it came to the part where Romeo commits suicide, Garth slid out of his desk chair and fell on the floor. He was good at reading, too. He would really help communicate the words. He got into it. That's one of the experiences that really stick out in my mind."

Woods recently reread one of Garth's essays from that ninth-grade class. "I keep papers that I like and sometimes pull them out and use them as examples for other classes," she said. The assignment was to write in the first person as an object of their choice. Garth became a trash can, imagining that he was eating the garbage as people disposed of it. "It was a good one," she said. "He had an active imagination, that's for sure."

One of Garth's favorite mentors at school was a counselor, Shelly Danner, who now lives near Charleston, West Virginia. Danner remembers Garth acting as a Fig Newton.

Garth regularly dropped in to visit with the counselor, not because he was a problem student or because of emotional distress. He just enjoyed talking with her and asking questions of an articulate young teacher.

"I'm just thrilled for him," Danner said. She's attended two of his concerts in the West Virginia area. The first time, Danner and one of Garth's former classmates, Debbie Holmes, went to the show early and spotted a former Yukon resident who works in Garth's concert crew. When Garth was told that they were in the audience, he immediately sent someone to bring them backstage. They visited before the show and for a long time after it was over. The next time, they returned for another friendly conversation.

"He has stayed as down-to-earth as he always has been," Danner said. "He's always been that way, just outgoing and personable. He hasn't changed."

In interviews Garth tends to downplay his youthful popularity or his status as a nice, personable fellow who worked hard to become a friend to everyone. He describes himself as a lazy sloth who didn't put much effort into anything. He didn't apply himself to his studies, he has said, and he wasn't a very good athlete.

His teachers remember him differently. But then, nice guys don't necessarily make for good quotes, and Garth has admitted that he has stretched the truth regularly during countless interviews over the last few years. His mother chides him for some of the stories she has read, saying she doesn't know where he comes up with such things.

Though hardly earth-shattering, Garth's biggest story reveals a guy who sometimes lets his imagination bend the facts too far. In an interview with a South Bend, Indiana, newspaper prior to a concert to raise funds for a federal law banning flag-burning, Garth told the reporter he'd been offered a partial athletic scholarship to join the famed Notre Dame football team. The Notre Dame athletic department, which maintains strict records about such offers, does not list a Garth Brooks from Yukon, Oklahoma, among those offered scholarships in the early 1980s. Nor does anyone at Yukon High recall him receiving such a prestigious invitation.

Anyone offered a scholarship, even a partial one, to an institution like Notre Dame would surely rate a full scholarship to a lesser school, such as Oklahoma State, where Garth enrolled after graduating from Yukon High in 1981. No athletic scholarships came Garth's way his last high school year, however. Not from Notre Dame, not from anywhere.

Not that his sports days were finished,

though. Competitor that he is, he was to make a name for himself at Oklahoma State, eventually earning a partial scholarship his sophomore year for track and field.

As for the Notre Dame boast, more than likely he simply slipped in an ill-considered white lie to impress a reporter who wasn't overly familiar with the singer. It was 1989, and he was still a new performer with little name recognition when he conducted the South Bend interview. The reporter apparently didn't bother to check the assertion. Garth often walks a line between boastful statements and a kind of self-criticism that doesn't seem completely honest. The young singer can be fairly transparent in attempting to present himself as a nobly humble person who downplays his past as well as his current accomplishments. He's a man unworthy of the attention and praise he receives, he repeatedly suggests. Maybe so, but he downplays his talents to a degree that doesn't represent his true feelings, either.

Asked about his high school days by *People* magazine, Garth blithely describes himself as "pretty much of a dick. Had to be the center of attention. Went from one girl to another. I was pretty shallow." His friends disagree. He probably would be surprised if they didn't.

Musically, his friends support his memories

of being someone who enjoyed a variety of popular styles. He was quick to pop tapes into cassette players in the car, and he enjoyed sitting around with friends listening to favorite tunes. His love for James Taylor was evident then, but he just as likely would lead a singalong to Boston's "More Than a Feeling" or Fleetwood Mac's "Go Your Own Way" during weekend get-togethers.

His leanings toward country music started to become evident in high school, despite the peer-consciousness of young adults of that age group. Garth entered a local talent contest while in the eleventh grade singing a country song. His fellow students hooted and laughed before he finished, then razzed him afterward for his choice. He never sang a country song in front of his classmates again—at least not for another decade.

However, during his final year at Yukon High, he now says he heard an album that changed his life. The album was *Strait Country*, and the song that affected him so strongly was a well-crafted, loosely swinging two-stepper titled "Unwound." Garth had discovered modern country music. Because of that, country music might never be the same.

Chapter
☆ 4 ☆

But country music was not the only musical style to influence Garth as a youngster. He began strumming an acoustic guitar with some conviction in junior high, slowly adding another instrument to already musical family gatherings. Still, like most men in junior high or high school in Oklahoma, he preferred sports to any other activity.

As Garth grew older he began to hear music beyond his parents' traditional country albums. He remembers hearing Tom Rush, Eric Andersen, Jimmy Buffett, the Allman Brothers, and the Marshall Tucker Band. Later his tastes grew to include melodic, slickly crafted rock music by Boston, Kansas, Journey, the Eagles, and other popular rockers of the time.

But his favorite artist early in his life was James Taylor. Throughout the late 1960s and 1970s, Taylor ranked as the preeminent singer-songwriter, a performer who blended sensitive, introspective lyrics and acoustic-based music with pop's melodic dynamics. He told tormented, confessional tales set with his understated tenor and a relaxed, intimate persona.

"His songs were as artful as they were emotional," wrote a *Rolling Stone* reviewer about Taylor's music. Those artful, emotional songs influenced a wide variety of performers, including a sensitive, rowdy athlete in Oklahoma named Garth Brooks.

These, plus many other styles, Garth says, helped shape him into a blend of hardcore country traditionalist and sensitive song-poet. More than fifteen years separate the oldest Brooks child from the youngest, so Garth was able to hear country music from the 1950s as well as the folk and rock of the 1970s that younger siblings brought home. "That probably is the reason for my diverse show on the stage," Garth has suggested. "There wasn't really a generation gap between parents and oldest brother so the music kept pouring down and down to me without losing an era somewhere."

Garth graciously cites his mother's influence upon him at every opportunity. "If I have any talent, it comes from her," he has said repeatedly. At the same time, neither Colleen nor Troy encouraged him to devote himself to music or show business. Their memories persuaded them to shield their children from the heartbreak of chasing a hard-to-attain dream.

"Mom tried to discourage our interest in music as a career," Garth has said. "She wanted something better for her kids." In another interview, he recalled talking directly to her about the ambitions that had been growing inside him. "Her advice was, 'Don't get in it,'" he remembered.

Garth's father gave him similar instructions about military service. As high school was nearing to a close, the singer told his father he was giving some thought to following in his footsteps and signing up with the Marine Corps. His father objected strongly, instead suggesting he attend college and develop a high-paying skill.

Nowadays the parents act mighty proud of their youngest child. But they also remind him to keep down to earth. His mother tells of his periodic trips to Yukon, where he takes a few days off and surrounds himself with what he calls "real people."

On his way back to the entertainment rocket ship to which he's now attached, his father usually meets him at the front door and, each time, offers him a variation of the same advice. "You know you're not living in the real world, don't you?" his father will tell him. Garth will smile, hug his father, and say, "Yeah, Dad, I know."

Chapter

☆ 5 ☆

Oklahoma State University got what the
Marine Corps didn't. It's unknown if his
father's experience as a marine affected his
decision, but Garth typified an OSU student.
He struggled to support himself with a combination of grants, financial assistance from his
parents, and working odd jobs. He delivered
pizza, sold shoes, worked as a nightclub door
attendant and bouncer. He lived in the dorm for
a while, and he also roomed with his brother, a
relationship that his friends later would remember as unusual. "It wasn't like Kelly was
helping out his little brother by giving him a
place to stay," said a close friend, Mike Wood.
"Those two were really close. They hung out
together. It's pretty amazing to see two brothers

be such good friends to each other. I don't think I've seen anything like it."

Garth enrolled as a marketing and advertising major, later saying he hoped to use his interest in music to find jobs creating jingles. As in high school, he's remembered as an above average student who worked hard and showed a lot of initiative. He was an inquisitive student who seemed to enjoy school more as he advanced.

His college friends remember Garth Brooks as an athlete, not an artist. A measure of how carefully Garth studies his options before making a decision can be found in the sport he pursued at OSU.

Though an accomplished football player, he realized he wasn't big enough physically to return to his position as a tight end, and his talent as a quarterback didn't rate very highly against the recruits the team had found for that highly valued spot in the lineup. Garth decided against trying out for that team.

The baseball squad seemed a little more likely, but he didn't pursue this option very far.

That left track and field. With 185 pounds spread thickly across a six-foot frame, he wasn't about to compete with the speed demons or the distance runners. Though he has a strong upper body and even stronger legs, he wasn't developed enough to throw the shotput or hurl the discus. And his squat stature didn't lend itself to jumping far or leaping high.

But he always had a good arm. He'd been a quarterback, a baseball pitcher, and an accurate, hard thrower as a baseball outfielder. After a talk with an assistant coach, he decided to try his luck at javelin. At Yukon, this Greek-inspired competition didn't exist. At OSU, however, Garth had found a sport to fit his physical makeup. Javelin tossing requires strong legs, good coordination, and most of all, a powerful and fast arm.

Garth chose the sport because it allowed him to continue to compete, albeit in a field with few takers. Nonetheless, he worked hard at developing his skill. Through weight training, he added twenty pounds of muscle while an athlete at OSU, eventually bench-pressing nearly 350 pounds. He still tells a joke he no doubt developed early in his years at Oklahoma State. Since being a javelin thrower surely brought questions and comments from peers, he quickly memorized a good javelin joke. "After a couple of years of catching it, they allow you to throw it," is a quip his friends recall him using, and it's one he continues to use today.

Despite the jokes, Garth proved good enough at the sport to become one of two javelin throwers to receive a partial scholarship at OSU, and he would go on to become a four-year letterman at the school.

His coach, Jim Bolding, maintains that Garth continued to act as personable in college as he had in high school. "He was real well-liked by his peer group and real down-to-earth," Bolding said. "He was a real down-to-earth fella, and he seems to have kept that when I've talked to him since then. He was a reasonably good javelin thrower, too. He couldn't have competed on a national level, but within our conference he was competitive."

He also remembers his student as a hard worker who pushed himself in several directions. "He was balancing school work with track practice and playing clubs in and around Stillwater," Bolding noted. "It put an extra depletion on him. He would show up a lot of the time with bags under his eyes. But he never asked for special treatment."

At times, Garth led the hijinks that normally take place on long bus trips with the track team. But toward the end of his college years, he would spend more and more time catching up on sleep while lying on top of suitcases at the back of the bus.

Mike Wood was among Garth's wide circle of friends at OSU. A long-distance runner who starred on the track squad, Wood roomed next door to Garth for a long spell in the OSU athlete's dormitory. A Michigan native, Wood still vividly recalls how struck he was by the genuine friendliness of Southerners.

"Garth was typical of the guys I met there," said Wood, who now operates a bike store back in Michigan. "He was very, very friendly, which was a whole different attitude from the people in the North. He just immediately treated me like he had known me for a long time. We had a lot of fun together. I saw him recently after a concert he had up here, and my friends were in awe. [They said,] 'Gosh, you know this big, famous star.' But he still has that same way of treating people. He hasn't changed much from that good ol' boy I knew in college."

Wood remembers Garth being more interested in what life was like in Michigan than most of the other track performers in their circle. "We got to know each real well because, besides the track stuff, we had a lot of classes together," Wood remembered. "We liked to blow off classes and go sit on the wall by the library and watch the girls go by."

The two friends ran with a fairly wild crew, but Garth was among the more mature members of the bunch. "Garth never drank, or at least he never drank much," Wood said. "I never saw him go out and get plowed, and I can't think of too many others I can say that about.

"He loved to go out with the guys, though, and he'd get as rowdy as anybody, but he never got sloppy or drunk. He knew how to enjoy himself, though. He'd dance, tell the best stories, flirt with the best girls. Women were attracted to him. He had a lot of girlfriends, until he met Sandy about midway through college. That settled him right down."

The most traumatic event for Garth, Wood, and their friends was the death of Jim Kelley, a track assistant who befriended many of the athletes. Garth and Kelley had grown to be close buddies.

"I remember this real clear," Wood said. "When we heard about Kelley's death, we were all stunned. It was like nobody could react. But Garth walked out and hit the wall a couple of times with his fist, and he broke his hand. Everyone was upset, but to see that kind of emotion. . . . It was amazing, I'll say that. Most of us had been taught to hide our emotions. But Garth was a real open guy. You always knew how he felt."

When Wood first heard that a guy named Garth Brooks had recorded a country album, he wondered if it was his old college buddy. When he first saw the album cover, he wasn't sure.

The Garth he knew always had a beard or a moustache, and his hair wasn't as neatly trimmed. He'd put on a little weight, too. Then he opened the album and saw that it was dedicated to Jim Kelley. He knew then that it was the same Garth.

Wood doesn't suggest that Garth is out of character in the cowboy hat, boots, striped dress shirt, and pressed denim trousers. In college, Garth's preferred daily wear consisted of cotton T-shirts, sweat pants, and gym shoes, with perhaps a ball cap on his head. "But when he went out, he put on the boots and the dress cowboy hat," Wood said. "He'd wear pretty much the same clothes he wears on stage now."

Garth was unique, Wood said, and a heck of a guy to know, especially for a stranger visiting a new region for the first time. "I'll tell you something about Garth," Wood concluded. "He could run faster than anybody I know in cowboy boots. I was a runner, and I was faster than him on the track. But if we both had cowboy boots, he was the fastest. He could scoot in those things. I'd never seen anything like it."

For an OSU athlete like Garth Brooks or Mike Wood, the immediate goal was to earn a berth in the track-and-field finals of the Big

Eight conference, to which OSU belonged. Garth competed in the javelin finals in his sophomore and junior years. He came close his senior year, but failed.

On the day he didn't qualify, he lay dejectedly on the foam rubber of the high-jump pit at Nebraska University. An OSU coach paraded by and told him, "Well, now you can get on with what you really want to do." Garth, who hates criticism as much as he hates to lose, was near tears at the time.

But, as much as the words hurt him, he took them to heart and remembers them to this day. After focusing most of his energy at excelling at any and all sports for most of his life, this taste of failure still lingers bitterly in his mouth.

In recalling the incident, he now says he can't understand why anyone would devote their lives to sports. In one interview, he said, "I couldn't understand why anybody would dedicate their life and time to something like sports. I just couldn't understand it. I would see these javelin throwers come in and train hundreds of hours a week."

In another interview in 1989, he broached the same subject. "I met a lot of kids there who I considered great athletes, and I saw how good they were and how hard they trained. As much as I admired them, I couldn't understand how someone could dedicate their life so much to one thing. One day I looked at myself out here in Nashville and felt real good about myself because I was dedicating all my time and efforts to music. It made me feel proud."

These days, he regularly cites that incident on the high-jump mat as a turning point. "A big bell went off and said, 'Hey, man, you're terrible at athletics, you're terrible at college. But the one thing you're proud to put your name to is your music. Maybe that's what the good Lord wants you to do."

He feels better about music, it seems, because he has made the division finals. He's a champion, at least for the time being. As with an athlete, coming in first is an accomplishment few have enjoyed, and it's something they can never take away from him. But it took realizing his accomplishments in sports were over before he could recognize music was the field where his opportunities were waiting.

When talking about the music he listened to in college, Garth sometimes will mention rock bands. It's almost always the same list: Boston, Kansas, Fleetwood Mac, and Journey. Sometimes he'll throw in a curve, such as

Kiss, but only to mention their stage show and how they entertained people. It's hard to imagine a moralist like Garth cranking up tapes by Black Sabbath or Led Zeppelin while in high school, or dancing to the Talking Heads and the Ramones, for that matter. His tastes paddled right down the mainstream.

In these musical discussions, Garth grows most passionate about lyricists. He'll mention the literate collaborations of Bernie Taupin and Elton John, the elliptical verse of Don McLean, and the introspective tunes of Jackson Browne. But, always, he returns to the man he describes as Sweet Baby James, better known as James Taylor. In college, however, he picked up another idol that he rates on the same level as Taylor. That writer-performer is Dan Fogelberg, who, like Taylor, writes blues-tinged acoustic pop music with a self-confessional air and a strong undercurrent of melancholy.

"I'm a big lyrics fan," Garth has said. "The lyrics of the James Taylors and the Dan Fogelbergs just kill me."

"It's also my dream to work with them sometime," Garth said in a 1989 interview. "Working with those two guys is almost as big as my dream of singing with George Jones."

Garth started performing more earnestly

in campus cafes and retaurants near campus, primarily covering songs by his folk-pop idols. "I realized that I got a lot more happiness playing six nights a week at a pizza parlor than I did playing sports," the singer has said. "I spend all day trying to write a song, and loving it the whole time. So I figured, 'Why not take this more seriously?' "

In 1984 he showed up at an audition that the Nashville-based Opryland USA theme park was holding in Oklahoma City. Garth showed up in boots and cowboy hat and thoroughly impressed the talent scouts. They offered him a job performing well-known country songs at the park, a job that would last through the summer and offer him a chance to gain exposure in a town known as Music City, USA.

He hadn't earned his degree in advertising and marketing yet, though. When Garth disagreed with his parents' suggestion that he wait until he finished college, Raymond Brooks decided to put his foot down and forbid that his son make the trip. Garth obeyed him.

"We made a deal," said Garth. He would stay in school. Once he received his degree, however, he would have their support and encouragement to pursue a musical career.

Meanwhile, his interest in country music

continued to grow. His appreciation of George Strait grew stronger with each new album issued by the quiet Texan. In addition, Garth was rediscovering albums by Merle Haggard and George Jones that he had heard his parents play over and over again as a child. Now, he realized, he had a new awareness of what the men were saying, and he savored their ability to gently probe such deep emotions.

He also began surveying his possibilities of actually earning a living performing music. He had his degree in advertising to fall back upon, knowing he could enter the jingle business if he failed as an artist who performed original material.

As he eyed the rock world, he saw little recognition any more for the type of lyric-based, gentle pop music he enjoyed and performed. Taylor and Fogelberg had become nostalgia acts in the 1980s; they no longer were putting new songs on the radio or talking directly to younger people. Dance, rap, and melodic hard rock by guys with carefully moussed long locks were dominating the pop charts. Radio and record companies didn't seem to want to promote sensitive songs anymore, and the successes of Suzanne Vega, Tracy Chapman, and the Indigo Girls were still a couple of years in the future.

"I found that the James Taylors and the Dan Fogelbergs weren't respected as much as they used to be," Garth has told reporters. "People didn't take heed and listen to them as much. Taylor and Fogelberg were trailblazers, and they had a cult following, but I didn't want to work that hard. I wanted to go where lyrics could be heard and the words meant something, and that was country music. I've always loved country music because it allows the words to say something. I don't think there's any style better than country music as far as letting the lyrics stand out as much."

He started plotting for his move toward country music long before graduation day. He received his diploma wearing cowboy boots underneath the robe. He had been reading endless stories about how George Strait, Ricky Skaggs, and Reba McEntire were transforming country music and how the music was evolving from older legends to fresh, younger faces.

He felt ready to go, and he felt sure Nashville would be ready for him when he arrived. There was only one person he hadn't settled the score with yet: his girlfriend, Sandy Mahl.

Chapter

☆ 6 ☆

Tumbleweeds was a favorite hangout for young OSU students, a place where Garth, his brother Kelly, and several of his friends from the track team would hang out on Friday nights.

As usual, Garth made his presence known whenever he dropped by. Within a few visits, he was friends with the doorman, the bartender, the band, the owners. He'd greet them by their first name, and before leaving, he would have spent time with each of them catching up on their lives. He was well-liked there, as everywhere else.

One night, Garth jumped in to help break up a fight. It didn't take much, but he helped pull one lug off of another, then shouted one of them down when the guy started threatening his opponent. Garth could grow real commanding fast, his friends say. He wasn't afraid to stick his nose directly in someone's face and tell them what he thought needed to be said, whether it was scolding a teammate for not giving 100 percent or talking down a couple of friends who were exchanging heated words.

When Tumbleweeds needed a new bouncer, the club manager thought of Garth. He offered him the job, and the young javelin thrower figured it beat making pizzas or selling shoes, his previous jobs near campus. The club employees trusted him. They knew he wasn't much of a drinker, so they didn't have to worry about him sneaking shots through the night and getting out-of-hand. He knew a lot of the students and was well liked and respected. He could handle a crisis with a sense of humor and didn't lose his head easily. He was a good man for the job.

The job never proved too dangerous, as his parents had worried it might. He broke up a few fights, but usually at least one of the guys was drunk and it didn't take much to pull them apart. Oklahomans tend to be civilized about their fisticuffs, too. They fight hard and more than most, but when an authority figure steps in to separate it, they usually stop. Most fistfights in bars don't last long, anyway. The two will end up tangled on the floor within a blow or two, and it's hard to do much damage at a horizontal angle. As often as not, a friend or fellow patron will step in before the action develops too far.

It was nearing closing time one weekend night when Garth was told a ruckus was unfolding in the women's bathroom. That drew a good chuckle from Garth and a few other guys, but after shrugging his shoulders, he shot in there to investigate.

A tall, tanned, shapely blond in a cowboy hat and tight jeans stood with her right fist lodged into the cheap, pressed plywood wall. She looked at Garth, who stood there with his eyebrows raised and his mouth caught between a smile and simply hanging wide open in disbelief. Garth also noticed a smaller, dark-haired young woman huddled in a corner. "What happened in here?" Garth asked. Sandy said, "I missed," shrugged, and smiled.

Garth instructed them both to leave. As it turned out, the other woman had accused Sandy of spending time with her boyfriend. One thing led to another, and Sandy, a former barrel racer in rodeo competition, decided to take action. "I was just trying to scare her," she later described it.

Garth told the woman in the corner she would have to leave the premises. Once the dust had settled slightly, Garth helped pry Sandy's hand from the wall and told her in much more friendly tones that she, too, would have to go. He also said it was club policy for him to escort her outside.

As they talked, he grew more and more interested in this feisty, tough-talking woman. Once outside, he told her the nightclub had another policy, that any bouncer who threw a woman out of the club also had to escort her home to make sure she made it safely. Sandy agreed but wasn't overly friendly about it.

On the ride home, Garth discovered Sandy was a former rodeo champion now attending Oklahoma State. She was three years younger than he was, but she had plenty of maturity and more spirit than any woman he had met.

Sandy lived in the college dormitory. Garth lived about two blocks away in an apartment he shared with his brother. "Look, my roommate's gone for the weekend. Why don't you come on up, and I'll drive you home in the morning?" he suggested.

Sandy didn't take long to think it over. "Drop dead, asshole," she replied. Garth still laughs every time he tells the story, and he tells it often. "That was all she said. I thought, 'This

girl's got class.' " In another interview, he said
he couldn't keep his mind off of her. He ap-
proached her in a more respectable fashion the
following day, calling and asking for a date. She
took him up on it.

Years later, Sandy would also remember
their unusual introduction and credit her tough
demeanor as one of the reasons Garth became
interested in her. "I turned him down," Sandy
told a reporter. "I think that's what caught his
eye."

Sandy Mahl was born in the tiny Oklahoma
town of Owasso, where residents remember her
as a popular, attractive student who was a
cheerleader during the school year and a life-
guard at the city swimming pool in the
summer. She also loved horses. She moved to
Stillwater to attend Oklahoma State shortly
after she graduated from Owasso High School
in 1983.

Garth's friends describe him as a polite
womanizer in college. The young women were
drawn by his charisma, his gentlemanly man-
ners, his friendly banter, and his intensity. He
dated several women in those years. From the
start, he took Sandy more seriously than the
others. He settled down quickly. "He'd still talk
about a girl being pretty or stuff like that,"
recalled his friend Mike Wood. "But, as far as

flirting, he just stopped it completely. He wouldn't have anything to do with other women after he met Sandy, not that I know about. He had always been the first one to make a move when we'd go out. But, once Sandy came along, he was a changed man."

He informed her of his plans to pursue a country music career. But he kept the part about leaving her behind in Stillwater a mystery until shortly before he left. He hinted that he might be back for her. However, he told her that if her demands got in the way of his mission to make it in country music, he would leave her behind in a flash.

"I was a jerk," he later admitted to an interviewer. "When I left, I didn't tell her, but I wasn't planning on coming back. I didn't think I'd see her again once I moved to Nashville."

Chapter

☆ 7 ☆

Deciding to leave Stillwater isn't the bold decision it may seem on the surface. After all, Stillwater is a college town: Five thousand or so residents leave every year; a few months later a few thousand more arrive.

"It's kind of bad form to stay there after graduation," said Mike Wood. "You're supposed to leave. You might go back to where you're from. You might move to a big city or wherever it is you're going to seek your career. But you don't stay."

Nonetheless, Garth had become a popular local performer. When he set a date to depart in the summer of 1985, he turned it into a celebration and a going-away party. He was setting off to become a star, and he invited everyone to come christen his starbound cruise. He left town puffed up with anticipation.

Arriving alone in Nashville, he pulled into a Holiday Inn on West End Avenue. The hotel was located near the famed Music Row area of Nashville, a sedate, low-key row of new office buildings and old homes renovated into business centers where nearly all of the country music industry is located. A row of neon-lit tourist traps and trinket centers were located not far from the hotel or from the business center, too. But the true places of power existed in stately decorated buildings with tastefully corporate signs out front that quietly but firmly stated such business names as Sony, BMG, Warner Brothers, MCA, Capitol, BMI, ASCAP, EMI, Arista, and so on. One building housed Randy Travis's management and promotion business, the next the people behind Alan Jackson. Down the street were the people who promote records to radio or try to get the names of the stars in major magazines and their faces on television shows.

Brooks wanted to join the stories that made Nashville famous. He probably already knew that Kris Kristofferson came to town a Rhodes Scholar and spent months sweeping floors as a janitor at a recording studio; that George Jones gave up his house-painting job to move here in the 1950s; that Loretta Lynn and her husband drove from the state of Washington while sleeping at night in their car in order to take a self-made single to WSM Radio.

But those stars arrived in old Nashville. The town is vastly different today, but Garth drove here with the same dream as his predecessors. He may have entered just as the country music business was undergoing revolutionary changes in leadership, vision, and conduct. But, in the long run, he was looking for the same thing every other singer came here to find: He wanted to make a name for himself in the entertainment business. He wanted to speak to people as James Taylor and Dan Fogelberg had spoken to him. When people heard the name Garth Brooks, he wanted them to gasp and gape.

Singer Loretta Lynn, in her best-selling biography *Coal Miner's Daughter*, said that, in country music, "The secret is getting loyal fans. . . . Once they like you, it's for life." Garth hoped to test that truism.

A friend had already set up an interview with Merlin Littlefield, vice president at ASCAP, an agency that collects fees from radio and other music users and disperses it to those who own the copyrights of the songs. ASCAP and BMI, the two leading performance rights agencies, act as a central power source in Nashville. Garth hoped to gain some advice from Littlefield and perhaps gain a recommendation. If Littlefield calls an artist manager, a record company talent scout, or a music publisher, they usually listen. It can be the introduction every dream-filled newcomer desires.

Littlefield listened to Garth's tape. His enthusiasm was, well, underwhelming. He explained to Garth just how slim his chances were. Thousands of young people just like him show up in town every year, and only a handful ever get to a level where they can earn even a poor living at writing or singing. It would take great determination on his part, and he still might not ever get a break. The majority of writers and singers, even those with talent who break into the business, still don't make much money.

As they spoke, a songwriter whose name Garth recognized stepped into the room. Littlefield recited a few of the fellow's hits. The guy had dropped in to ask for a loan. He needed five hundred dollars pronto or the bank would foreclose. He sounded and acted desperate.

"I was this kid who had never been out of Oklahoma, and I thought all I had to do was open my guitar case and start singing and everything else would fall into place," Garth has said about his initial visit to Nashville. "I thought I was all set up, I was going to be a star. I got out here and found out that I'd certainly blown it all out of proportion. I was very scared, depressed, and shocked."

He has called the appearance of the veteran songwriter "a God-given sign to me while I was sitting in that office. I saw this guy come in, a guy I knew was a really great songwriter, and he couldn't pay off a five-hundred-dollar loan. I looked at him and said, 'I make that much in a week just playing nights in Oklahoma.' This guy in the office said, 'Then go home.' At the time, I hated him for saying it, but now I secretly thank him every day for setting me straight."

To a different reporter, Garth expanded on his feelings on that fateful day. "They told me a person never gets rich just being a songwriter or an artist, and it was like a mirror dropped on the ground and shattered. I was sure that everybody in that building could hear my heart break. So I just stood up and told myself, 'I was a fool to come all the way out here, but I'll be damned if I'm fool enough to stay."

Garth remembers striding out of the room angrily, busting forcefully through the heavy glass front doors of ASCAP's then headquarters at the corner of Seventeenth Avenue and Division Street. "I went back to my hotel room, went out on the balcony, and stood there in the pouring rain," he has said. "I felt so stupid and sad. It was like every raindrop was laughing at me."

That night, Garth stretched out on his bed for hours, without reading, watching television, or falling asleep. "When you are by yourself for the first time, you really have to prove yourself. You start looking down inside you, about what makes you up. You start pulling these things out to handle each adversity as it comes. I took a real good look as to who I was for the first time. I was made up of my family, the good Lord, and my friends. None of them were around me. There was something that kept me saying, that is what I'm supposed to do, but the time sure wasn't right. I was sitting looking at those motel walls. I made up my mind, I'm going home."

Looking back, Garth has explained his emotional reaction to his first brush with discouraging words. "Nashville screams for commitment. Everybody I talked to asked, 'How long do you plan to stay in town?' I had this big fear about the work commitment. Commitment had been like a four-letter word to me my whole life. The idea of being committed to something or someone scared me to death. Since then, I've learned that a man can reach higher when he's tied down than he can when he's free."

He still gets philosophical about that first visit. "Yeah, there's nothing like an idiot with confidence. I came here thinking that country music needed me, that there was a hole in country music that I could fill. I didn't dream there would be a million other people thinking the same thing. I was shocked by the sadness in singing music. There's ninety percent sadness and ten percent happiness in this town. I'm thankful that I had the common sense to realize that I wasn't supposed to be in Nashville at that time.

"That experience taught me one of the greatest lessons ever: You can't leave behind what makes you up, and that's what I thought I'd do. I left Oklahoma swearin' I wouldn't need anyone there again."

Garth didn't return to Stillwater. He was too embarrassed. "I just went back home and hid," he explained. "They'd had a big sendoff for me in Stillwater before I left, and I just couldn't go back and face those people."

His mother welcomed him home, consoling him while telling him it wasn't necessarily time to give up. "He got down there and they shut the door on him," she has said. "It wasn't failure. He just didn't know the ins and outs.

He wasn't ready. He had never really been away from home before, had never been alone."

Eventually, Garth licked his wounds, tucked in his tail, and returned to Stillwater. "I know that was tough on him," Mike Woods said. "You could tell he was hurting. But Garth is a real determined guy. He doesn't stay down too long."

Before long, Garth joined the remnants of a popular Stillwater group, the Skinner Brothers Band, which had recently broken up. Newly named Santa Fe, and featuring Garth as lead singer, the band soon proved highly popular throughout the Southwest, playing college bars and fraternity parties from Little Rock, Arkansas, to Phoenix, Arizona. The band mixed nostalgic rock hits by Bob Seger and Creedence Clearwater Revival with modern country hits by Strait, Travis, and Dwight Yoakam.

"During that time, I got to learn a lot of the business aspect of music," he told Jack Hurst of the *Chicago Tribune*. "I got into a couple of situations where the money wasn't there at the end of the gig, and I had to either fight or get walked on."

Within months of returning, he asked Sandy to marry him. The wedding took place in May 1986. She supported his musical work, but Garth still complained to her and his parents about the hard conditions of performing on the road, the long, late hours, and the poor arrangements for sound and stage in most of the places Santa Fe performed. "But that was different from now," his mom said in 1990. "They went around in vans and pickups. It was a tough life, but he toughed it out."

After a year of commitment to his marriage and a year of commitment to making Santa Fe successful, Garth believed he had conquered the fears that had held him back throughout his life.

"I think my fear of commitment has always been a fear of failure. When I was playing sports, I hopped around from football to basketball to baseball, never committing myself to one sport," he said. "I was the same way with my relationships with women and friends. It took a while for me to find out that commitment isn't that bad. In fact, it's really kind of nice."

He felt prepared to take another shot at the big time. This time, however, he wouldn't tackle it alone. He had Sandy's complete support; she told him she looked forward to living somewhere new with him and helping him chase his dream. Santa Fe had made a pact when they formed: When they had accomplished all that they could in Oklahoma, they would move on. About a year-and-a-half after they formed, Santa Fe decided they were ready to try Nashville. "Don't get me wrong: Nashville can be a cold city. It can tear your heart out and stomp on it," he related about the time he was leaving Oklahoma. "But this time I wasn't scared. I knew exactly what I wanted to do."

Chapter

☆ 8 ☆

Timing is everything, it has been said. When Garth returned to Nashville with his new band and his wife, the country music business was beginning to crawl out of one of its bleakest sales periods. Even the staid *New York Times* had earlier looked down upon the city long enough to create a front-page story declaring that the Nashville Sound was dead.

In a 1986 Harris survey on music preferences, more than half of the respondents said they listened to country music on the radio. Some 59 percent preferred country while rock drew 44 percent, classical 35 percent, and rhythm-and-blues 34 percent.

Country radio actually had grown in listeners for the previous two decades. In 1961, only

eighty-one full-time country music stations existed; by 1986, that number was 2,275. (Today
it's over 2,300.) The problem, however, wasn't
listenership, it was sales. People who listened
to country didn't flock to record stores in the
same way people who listened to rock, rhythm-
and-blues, and pop did. The country listener
tended to be older and less likely to spend
money on music; the rock listener was younger
and eager to stock up on albums.

Once Santa Fe settled in Nashville, they made
another pact: Each member would devote at
least six months to the group's effort to secure
a record contract or some kind of career step.
As with many groups featuring several willful
individuals trying to forge a democracy, it
didn't last as long as they promised.

"You stick five guys, two wives, a kid, and a
dog and a cat in one house, and try to see how
you deal with the unknown," Garth told a
Tulsa World reporter before the release of his
first album. "I'm telling you, it's scarier than
hell. On top of that, we all had our own different ways of dealing with things, and as a result,
everything just kind of fell apart. There were
some hard feelings, but not as many as you
might think. We're still interested in what the
other ones are doing. We still speak to each

other. But it was real scary. Nobody knew what was going on."

Still, though the group had broken up, Garth doggedly refused to sign any contracts until after the six-month period had passed.

He and Sandy stayed with Bob Childress for a spell. Childress, who is a successful Nashville songwriter, suggested that Garth needed to get out and meet some other writers and to circulate about town. He took him to the Bluebird Cafe to attend what is called a writer's night, where a successful songwriter introduces several promising up-and-comers. Everyone offers a few selections, gets a reaction, and listens to the rest of the bill.

The Bluebird, in some ways, may be to modern Nashville music what the Opry was to earlier generations. It's where performers, especially those who write and appreciate good lyrics, hang out and perform.

At first glance, it's about as unassuming as a nightclub can be. The stage is barely eight feet deep and a little more than twelve feet wide. Fewer than one hundred seats circle the small tables; no more than one hundred and fifty people can cram into the club's standing room. No dressing room exists.

Yet it's the creative center for the city's songwriting community. Newcomers dream of being invited on stage, and they line up by the hundreds for a shot at an audition. Veterans like Vince Gill, Kathy Mattea, and Rodney Crowell still drop in to perform, sometimes to pay homage and sometimes to rekindle a creative spark. It's a listening room in the best sense of the word.

Owner Amy Kurland opened the club in 1982, and the room's reputation rests on her taste and management style. Kurland does everything from book the nightly performances to hush customers who socialize too loudly during shows.

Garth and Childress attended a show by a highly literate, risk-taking songwriter named Kevin Welch. While there he met Stephanie Brown. "I actually went home with her that night, and we wrote some together," Garth has said. "The next night we got together to write, and she told me she knew somebody I needed to meet."

That somebody was Bob Doyle, at the time an executive at ASCAP. Garth surely experienced some mixed emotions walking into the ASCAP building, the scene of the nightmarish episode that ruined his initial visit to Nashville.

This time, however, the reaction was different. Doyle flipped for Garth's work. Doyle introduced Garth's music to several publishing companies and to numerous artist managers. A few were impressed, but all of them said they were too busy to take on another songwriter or another client.

Garth found himself fighting the same dark feelings of defeat that he had confronted during his initial visit. He asked Sandy if the couple shouldn't give it up and return to Oklahoma. "She just sat me down and said, 'Look, I was around when you came back the last time, and I'm not going through that again,' " Garth has said. " 'I think you're good enough and you think you're good enough, so we're going to stay right here. We'll get jobs, work, and live here and you'll work on your music.' "

One night, while driving home with Sandy from a frustrating outing, he stopped the car because he could no longer see through the tears of rage and frustration in his eyes. He stepped from the car and into a rainstorm, and he began shouting and beating his head against the car's roof.

"I thought we weren't going to make it," he told a reporter. "I thought we were going to crash, trash out, go into debt, poverty, all this stuff. It had nothing to do with the music; it was two people, newly married, struggling against debt. I thought it was over.

"When I was a quarter of a mile from my house—knocking myself in the head as hard as I could and my wife over there screaming and crying—little did I know that fifteen minutes later, when I walked in the house, we'd open the paper and find the perfect jobs that fed and housed us for a year and a half."

The advertisement was for jobs in a big Nashville cowboy boot store that sold big-name dress boots at a discount price. When Garth and Sandy showed up to apply for both positions, the owner immediately liked both of them. "I walked in the door and he said, 'You're hired,'" Garth said, embellishing the story with his characteristic flair for drama. "He was from Texas, and I'm from Oklahoma. He said Sandy and me looked like the kind of folks they had working back home."

The day after the six-month pledge to Santa Fe had expired, Garth signed a publishing contract with Bob Doyle. The ASCAP executive had not been able to find a company willing to back Garth. But, in a testament to his belief in the young Oklahoman, Doyle left ASCAP to start his own publishing firm. He signed Garth as his first client.

Doyle's new company, Major Bob Music, provided Garth with a monthly three-hundred-dollar stipend to write songs. Doyle also introduced him to other writers, including cowboy song-poet Larry Bastian. He also found Garth singing work on demonstration tapes put together by other songwriters. Many successful (and unsuccessful) songwriters aren't competent vocalists. After writing a song they often hire those who can sing to record the new works. These tapes are then given to producers, record company talent scouts, and others who look for new material for recording artists.

Garth also gained work as a jingle singer: His voice could be heard pitching Lone Star Beer and John Deere tractors and farm equipment in commercials recorded in 1987 and 1988. Again, Doyle helped land Garth the work, which helped pay bills and build confidence.

Meanwhile, Sandy worked hard at the boot store to help both of them maintain their jobs. Though Garth was manager, he often let Sandy run the store while he sat in back working on songs. If the store got busy, he'd come out to help. He also ran into town to sing or meet with cowriters while Sandy covered for him.

Doyle, a gentle and soft-spoken man with a sincere passion for good songwriting, still couldn't interest record companies or managers in his new client. He began thinking about managing Garth himself. He mentioned the idea to Pam Lewis, a veteran publicist who had worked at MTV during its startup before moving to Nashville to head the country publicity department at RCA Records. She clashed with the RCA brass, however, and soon started her own company, where she helped garner press coverage for renegade country acts Steve Earle, Lyle Lovett, and Townes Van Zandt. The two decided to start their own company, Doyle/Lewis Management. Garth was the first artist the two ever managed together.

"If we need a name for what we're doing, we could call it 'melting pot management,' " said Lewis, a witty and outspoken woman who combines New York brashness, New Age values, and a funky, frank individuality. "Garth, Bob, and I are a team. We all bring different skills and different perspectives. We run a pretty tight ship because we make it a point to cover all bases. We take the 'personal' in personal management seriously."

At the boot store, the gregarious Garth began meeting musicians, many of whom he liked immediately. He sold a pair of boots to James Garver, who now plays electric guitar in Garth's band. Garver brought Steve McClure by the store to meet Garth. McClure is now Stillwater's pedal-steel guitarist. McClure, to continue the pattern, introduced Garth to drummer Mike Palmer, another member of Stillwater.

The momentum seemed to build weekly. One of Nashville's most successful and respected record producers, Jerry Kennedy, saw a lot of promise in Garth when Doyle introduced the two. He agreed to record some songs with Garth to help him try to secure interest from talent scouts.

Kennedy, once an esteemed session guitarist, had helped shape the recordings of the Statler Brothers, Mel McDaniel, and many others. His tastes are tough and solid; by showing interest in Garth, he immediately upped his credibility within Nashville's inner circle of record-makers.

Garth was quickly gaining friends in high places. He was winding his way through the complex maze of contacts needed to gain the scantest of opportunities, and he was picking up speed as he moved along. The confidence he always had in himself was starting to be reflected by others. The second coming of Garth Brooks was working out much better than the first.

"You gotta be in the right place at the right time, but luck doesn't get you dick three or four albums down the line," Garth told a radio disc jockey in an unusable interview. "That's going to take work, which I'm willing to invest. I'm in it for the long haul, which is the way it should be."

Chapter

☆ 9 ☆

Garth signed a contract with Major Bob Music on November 16, 1987. In January 1988, he signed with Doyle/Lewis Management. In February, he was working with producer Jerry Kennedy.

By March, Kennedy had introduced him to Joe Harris, a veteran concert-booking agen7t who worked for Buddy Lee Attractions, one of Nashville's oldest and most successful agencies.

"Kennedy had told me about this new singer," Harris confirmed. "I told him to bring him up to the office. He did, and he brought his guitar along. He sat there and sang awhile. I was knocked out, and I noticed people from all over the office seemed to gravitate to my door.

You don't have to hit me too hard over the head for me to know something will work."

Harris assured the young singer that he would gain entrance into the hallowed corridors of a record company soon. He told him to remain patient and to keep working. "Joe told us no matter what record company we went with, he wanted to book me," Garth has said. The singer signed with Buddy Lee Atractions for concert booking, and he has remained with the company and with Harris since.

As Garth's profile grew within the music industry, his managers recommended that he keep a low profile in other areas. They told him not to play writer's nights or to try to perform in nightclubs around Nashville. "If you play too long at a club in this town, you'll become known as a club singer," he was told. Stop singing on demonstration tapes for other writers, too, he was instructed. "You don't want your voice to become known from demos, because you don't want the people at the record companies to get too familiar with your voice. You don't want to go in to try and get a record deal and have the guy say, 'Oh, yeah, I know your voice. I've heard it on the demos you've done.'"

Obviously, Garth had climbed high enough to start walking a fine line. He had gained enough exposure to attract some important attention; now his managers wanted to guide his exposure in certain calculated directions designed to have the greatest impact.

Doyle diligently sent the tape produced by Kennedy to several record company executives and producers. In one way or another, though, every major record company in Nashville said they weren't interested in Garth, at least not at the time.

But Doyle's doggedness eventually wore down an executive at Capitol Records. Lynn Shults, now a *Billboard* magazine executive, was head of Capitol's artist and repertoire division in 1988, meaning he was responsible for finding talent, developing artists' careers, and seeking out hit songs.

Shults was impressed with Doyle's enthusiasm for the young singer, and the involvement of Kennedy and Harris surely piqued his interest. Doyle suggsted something unusual: He wanted to bring Garth by to perform for Shults and Jim Fogelsong, then chief executive of Capitol's Nashville division.

"Not many people get that kind of audition," Shults said. "He was OK that day, but you could tell he was nervous as hell. He did about five or six songs, we talked a bit, and he left. Two or three weeks had passed, and we hadn't gotten back to him. It wasn't that we had decided to pass on it. We just hadn't discussed it any further at that point."

The lack of any official decision, though, is probably a moot point. If a company lets that much time pass after a high-profile, intimate audition, the lack of enthusiasm speaks loud and clear. They simply weren't too interested in Garth Brooks.

A few weeks later, Shults attended a special showcase at the Bluebird Cafe sponsored by the Nashville Entertainment Association. The NEA occasionally sponsors such shows, which present specially chosen new performers to talent scouts and record producers. Doyle suggested that Garth attend, and he drove him to the showcase so he could see who else was coming up in town.

Doyle and Garth both noticed Shults in the audience, as well as a few other people they wanted an opportunity to impress. When one of the performers didn't show, Doyle jumped up and suggested to the organizer that he had a young singer who could take the slot. Most volunteers would have been turned down, but Doyle's reputation won out. They figured the guy couldn't be too bad.

Garth ran out to his truck and grabbed his acoustic guitar. "He did two songs," Shults recalled. "One of them was 'If Tomorrow Never Comes.' He just nailed me to the wall, and everyone else in the room, too. I walked up to him and Bob right there at the Bluebird and told them that if you want it, you got a record deal right now as far as I'm concerned. As long as Jim Fogelsong doesn't kill it, we've got a deal. We shook hands right there."

The next morning, Shults entered Fogelsong's office, trying to concentrate on his enthusiasm and hide his nervousness about making such an offer. "I told him I had made a handshake agreement with Garth. He looked at me a little funny, and I told him he could override me, but that as far as I was concerned, this kid was the real deal and we should sign him right now. He said, 'Well, if you feel that strongly about it, yes, go ahead.'"

Garth had performed "If Tomorrow Never Comes" during his initial audition with Capitol. But what Shults missed was how focused and electrifying the singer becomes when delivering a song to an audience. His nervousness at Capitol kept him from connecting with his lyrics in the way he can when the elements are right. At the Bluebird, Garth communicated his lyrics with an intense gaze and subtle, powerful body movement. In concert, "If Tomorrow Never Comes" remains a dramatic masterpiece, and Shults caught the full effect inside the crowded Bluebird that April evening in 1988. Now he knew why Doyle was so excited about this stocky, cherub-faced Oklahoman.

When Garth and Doyle enthusiastically passed the good news along to Jerry Kennedy, the response was not what they expected. "When he heard I'd been signed to Capitol, he told me he didn't get along very well with the folks over there, and it would be best for me to find another producer," Garth admitted to *Performance* magazine. "I hated that because Jerry is a great guy, and I have a lot of respect for him. But I also respected his position."

Nonetheless, Garth and Doyle brought up Kennedy's name during an initial meeting that Shults set up to discuss possible record producers. Shults shook his head and made a few other suggestions he said would be more appropriate for Garth. Shults agreed to set meetings with seven producers.

The first meeting was with Allen Reynolds, another veteran Nashville producer whose work included many hits by Don Williams, Crystal Gayle, and Kathy Mattea. Reynolds is a laid-back, philosophical man known for establishing a good relationship with his artists. Reynolds, unlike some other Nashville producers, is known for working with singers to develop the sound they want rather than forcing his ideas and formulas on them. He's particularly good at crafting a mood that subtly brings out the drama in a song, as heard in his work on Crystal Gayle's "Don't It Make Your Brown Eyes Blue" or Kathy Mattea's "Where've You Been." He's also a risk-taker with a good ear for an unusually powerful song, and he will encourage his artists to take chances.

He and Garth hit it off immediately in that first meeting. Reynolds liked Garth's spunk and bald ambition; Garth responded to Reynolds's knowledge, musical suggestions, and willingness to listen. The choice of Reynolds as producer is as important as any other connection Garth made while preparing to leap into the big leagues. His records wouldn't sound the same without him.

An example of the magic of Garth and Reynolds make can best be discovered by comparing Garth's version of "Friends in Low Places" with a version recorded at about the same time by Mark Chesnutt for release on Chesnutt's debut album in 1990. Chesnutt's is slower, more conventional; Garth adds a stirring bit of drama to the opening verses and then, near the end, sends the song into an open, exhilarating celebration, complete with a rowdy male chorus. It's a masterpiece of how to pull out the stops and bring out the full emotional possibilities of a good song.

In one of the first sessions with Reynolds and engineer Mark Miller (who has worked on all three Garth Brooks albums), the singer and producer were discussing musical direction. Garth envisioned a sound blending Texas swing and honky-tonk with operatic-pop ballads. "I'm thinking of something between Gary Morris and a George Strait kind of thing."

The producer responded with some sage advice. "Look, you gotta be yourself. God has things meant for you to do, and if you're meant to do this business, you'll do it. Just be yourself."

Garth, in retelling the incident, contends that the meeting "turned my life around." He remembers starting a particular song by dropping into his voice and booming the opening lyrics with operatic fullness. Reynolds interrupted him and asked, "Hold it, wait a minute, what's this voice?" Again, it was Garth trying to mimic something that didn't come naturally to him or fit his style. He now considers it the best advice he's ever received as an artist.

"I tell that story to anyone I meet who's thinking of pursuing this dream," Garth has said. "My advice is, 'Hey, man, it's your dream. Everyone's got opinions. Take them with a grain of salt. Listen to the people who want to see you succeed, plus listen to the people who want to see you fail, because you can learn from both of them.' "

Garth also recites a bit of wisdom acquired from engineer Mark Miller. When he first heard it, Garth said it made so much sense that he nearly fell out of his chair. "He said each single should reveal a little about the singer to the listener," Garth told US magazine. "That's what I do."

As the team began preparing for the album, Garth was forced to let go of some songs he'd written that were special to him. One was called "Don't Forget Where You've Come From," a song about roots and family inspired by his first disastrous trip to Nashville and the lessons he learned; another was titled "Over Forty and Under the Gun," which described the dilemma of mid-life crisis.

But the singer and producer agreed on several other songs, including some that surprised Garth, such as "Much Too Young (To Feel This Damn Old)," a song he'd written with a Stillwater pal named Randy Taylor, who now works in the athletic department of the University of Kansas. Taylor brought the song to Garth during a show in Stillwater, and Garth helped finish it right there and performed it that night.

(When Garth called him to let him know it would be on the first album, Taylor said, "I just want a boat out of the deal." On January 1, 1990, shortly after receiving his first royalty check for radio airplay on the song, Taylor bought a boat.)

Garth later described the type of songs he wanted for his debut. "I had always thought that if I got the chance, I'd like to have a musical feel that really feels good to sit in— and then while you've got 'em there strapped in, feed 'em some opinions. With every song, you've got a chance to get on a soapbox and tell a nation something, and you might as well tell them something that needs to be said. If the songs are funny, I want them to be clever. If they're serious, I want them to be real deep, to reach in there and try to grab you by the heart."

Chapter
☆ 10 ☆

Garth Brooks didn't mature into a dynamic entertainer: He started out that way. Speak to anyone about his ability to perform at any level of his career—from college nightclub attendees to fellow Nashville songwriters to Southern honky-tonk owners to the tens of thousands who attend arena shows today—and they all sweep into superlatives about his intensity, energy, and charisma.

He talks volumes about songwriting and the message he wants to communicate and about arrangements and his desire to experiment and push country's boundaries. But, in truth, the truly remarkable aspect of his talent is his complete lack of inhibition on stage. That trait is rare, especially in country music.

Lynn Shults remembers traveling through Alabama to attend Garth's earliest concerts on the Southern honky-tonk circuit. In Montgomery, Alabama, only six people sat in the audience for one of Garth's first concerts with Stillwater. The second night, in Birmingham, the crowd grew to thirty people.

Each night, though, Garth and his bandmates performed with abandon. "It was just one hell of a show," Shults recalled. "It was evident that he was heads-and-shoulders above anybody in country music as far as what he gave the crowd. The place just went bonkers. There were these two women, very attractive, and they shouted and danced and reacted to everything the band did. Garth jumped down onto the floor and danced with them. He had everyone in the place going. The club owner came over and said, 'I don't care if I am losing my ass, I'm having this guy back.' "

According to reports, that was one of the tamer shows on the tour. Garth has stepped out ready to conquer the world nightly in more than four hundred concerts over the past two years. He wasn't satisfied unless the crowd screamed with him on the up-tempo songs and cried on the ballads. In assessing his growing fame, comanager Pam Lewis has credited his showmanship as the link that led to his attracting fans in numbers far beyond other country stars.

When recruiting his band, the singer put enthusiasm beyond technique. "I don't know how good you have to be to play the same music every night, but you have to contribute to the enthusiasm we try to generate," he said.

A requirement for joining the initial band was a willingness to hang out together for several weeks before the first tour began. They attended movies together, shot pool, organized dinners and picnics. Garth wanted to know the group could play together off-stage as well as on. "Chemistry is the most essential element in a good band," he said.

Today, all but one of his original band members make up Stillwater. As of October 1991, the group includes Dave Gant on keyboards and fiddle; Steve McClure and James Garver on electric guitars; Mike Palmer on drums; Ty England, an old buddy from Stillwater, on acoustic guitar and vocals; and Betsy Smittle on bass.

His concerts, he contends, are the only place a listener can get the full effect of his music. "In my opinion, cutting records and performing concerts should be as far apart as day and night. If you want to hear the record note for note, stay home and listen to it on the stereo. In concert, the ballads are done slower and the upbeat songs are done quicker. We're a lot louder, and it's pretty much a wonderful, fun night of cowboy rock 'n' roll. We've been known to bust a guitar and dance on a few tables."

He also enjoys performing as much as any aspect of being a musical artist. "I'll look up and get this feeling, 'Man, I hope this is what the good Lord has intended for me to do all my life, because I sure like it.' On stage is where my heart beats fastest and the wildest that my blood rushes. There's nothing like when the crowd is into it and you're just nailing it."

Recently, Garth has begun comparing a good concert to good sex, "where you get wild and frenzied, then turn around quick to something gentle, tender, and slow, and then get wild and crazy again and just keep doing that over and over until one of you drops dead. It's the same great, physical thing with the music, and it happens every night."

During the first few months of touring, he admits his sexual bravado sometimes continued after the shows. "At first, I reacted like ninety-five percent of the people would. I went nuts, staying up all night, trying to be up twenty-six, twenty-seven hours straight. I didn't want to miss anything. My wife said, 'You're gonna kill yourself, and I'm not going to stick around to see it.' I thought for some time I might lose it. I calmed my act down. I try to take it all in stride, and handle it as best as I can. It's a huge temptation, though."

The partying included dalliances with women, he has admitted. "All of a sudden I had all these women right there in my lap." It started early on, as women would move beyond asking him to autograph pieces of paper or pictures to asking him to sign body parts. "Beautiful women, women I thought were unreal, would walk up to me and say, 'Sign this.' Only there was nothing in their hands," Garth told a reporter. "So I just dove in and had a blast."

When Sandy first viewed him signing his name on a woman's body at an Abilene concert, she exploded in anger. "She was furious," Garth said. "She told me, 'These people have no respect for me whatsoever, and it's because of you.' Her words pretty much hit me between the eyes and made me wake up, and I realized she was right." He admitted his behavior was wrong.

Sandy also once pulled a woman from a stage and threw her across a table at one of Garth's concerts. The woman had climbed up and started dancing seductively with Garth as he sang. "When Sandy gets mad, she counts to herself, and I can usually pick it up at about six or seven," the singer explained to *Chicago Tribune* reporter Jack Hurst. "One night this little gal was drunk and singing on the microphone, trying to get as close to me as she could, and I looked out there and Sandy was on three. I thought, 'Oh, God.'

"I tried to figure out what to do, but she didn't even get to five, she just stood up, and even though this little gal on stage was pretty good-sized, Sandy grabbed her by the shoulders and threw her off the front of the stage and over the first table."

During that first year of touring, Garth would sometimes go almost a week without contacting Sandy or letting her know where he was. Eventually, through an informant, Sandy discovered that her fears were true, that her husband had been unfaithful. She phoned to tell him her bags were packed.

"Garth was crushed," his friend Ty England told *People* magazine. "He pretty well lost it and choked up during the chorus of 'If Tomorrow Never Comes.' That night changed all our lives. We saw how much we could hurt somebody. Garth has said to me a million times that was probably the best thing that ever happened to him."

It took time for Sandy to rebound from her

pain, she said. But Garth had returned home, dropped to his knees, and cried while begging her to stay. Since then, he has said, "It took a hell of a human being to forgive me. I had to promise I'd make this marriage work. It ain't a bed of roses now, but we bust our asses, and it works unbelievably well."

On the road, Garth says the band members help keep each other in line, sidling up to one another whenever one starts to flirt or appears to be getting involved with someone else.

Still, Garth complains about having to be away from his wife for long periods of time. "I had this idea that after I had a hit record, I could afford to fly home a lot or bring her on the road with me whenever I wanted." She visits him regularly, but the road isn't something someone travels for fun.

The wild parties and one-night stands had ended before Garth started selling records in massive numbers. He credits his wife for making him understand what was important and setting his priorities straight. "She's been the difference," Garth told *Country Music* magazine.

Among the shows that first year was one Garth's hometown of Yukon will never forget. About the time his initial single, "Much Too Young (To Feel This Damn Old)," was climbing the charts, the Yukon chapter of the Future Farmers of America decided to see if they could pay for him to come to town for a fundraising concert. The show took place in the fall after Garth had achieved a few hits.

That day, Garth visited the campus, asked about his former teachers, and played some basketball with band members in the gymnasium. Verlin Goodson, an agriculture teacher and one of the concert organizers, remembers Garth pulling a young girl from the crowd during "If Tomorrow Never Comes," as well as how gracious Garth acted throughout the event. "He was very nervous before the show," Goodson remembered. "He wasn't sure if people were going to like him or not."

They did. After the show, when the head of a parents' organization presented him with his $7,500 check for performing, Garth tore it up and tossed it. He then stayed until 1:45 A.M. signing every autograph and posing for every picture. He had an excuse to leave earlier, Goodson said; the curfew for the gym was midnight. But when Garth was told he said he wasn't leaving until he was finished with the fans. They could go ahead and turn out the lights, he said, but he was staying.

He has had his bad moments on stage in the last two years, too. There was the night he fell into the orchestra pit at the Concord Pavillion in Northern California. And there was the night he stopped a song to shout at security for not stopping a guy carrying a video camera in front of the stage, only to discover the cameraman was part of the auditorium crew and that his camera work was being projected live on large screens on the side of the stage.

The stage, though, is where Garth celebrates his talents with a visceral energy that separates him from other performers. To watch him is to know why he has sold eight million albums in two years. To watch him is to know why, despite his lack of experience, he became the youngest person to become country music's reigning Entertainer of the Year.

Chapter
☆ 11 ☆

The Bluebird Cafe in Nashville not only played a prominent role in Garth receiving his record contract; it's also where he first heard the most important song on his first album.

Garth was sitting in at the Bluebird listening to a string of songwriters perform, including Tony Arata, a gentle, curly-haired Georgian with wire-rim glasses and a professional air. Arata carries himself with the humble gentility of a priest, and his songs are introspective and ripe with morals and messages. Like Garth, he seems inspired by the sensitive folk-pop poets of the 1970s; unlike Garth, he doesn't look like someone who would be comfortable in a ten-gallon hat or a guy who would push himself to the front row of a Boston concert.

Arata had been living in Savannah, Georgia, and performing acoustic solo sets in coffeehouses when Jim Glaser made one of his songs a Top Ten country hit. Before long, Arata was living in Nashville, performing and writing as he had in Savannah, but playing for a completely different audience. In Nashville his audience includes record producers, music publishers, and artists, some of them unknown, as Garth Brooks was when he first heard Arata perform "The Dance" in 1988.

Brooks vividly remembers hearing the song for the first time. The song is about someone reflecting back on a relationship that has ended. It's left open whether it ended because of death or other reasons, but the singer is glad they enjoyed the good times, not knowing they'd be short.

The natural reaction would be to think the lyrics are about a couple, though they just as easily could be about a family or friend. Garth, however, had a different reaction. The first time he heard it, he said, "I thought of Martin Luther King and John Kennedy."

Garth gave a tape of songs that included "The Dance" to Reynolds in one of their initial meetings. It fit his criteria for what he wanted on the first album. As he said at the time of its release, "I hate ear candy. You can write it and make a living. But I want to get below the surface, to reach the heart of the listener. If you can't bring a tear, make someone smile, or change their life in some way, why write it?"

Over the next few weeks, he passed several tapes to Reynolds, all for the sake of discussion about what should appear on his debut. When Reynolds brought up the song later, Garth resisted. By then, the album was taking on a traditional country flavor, complete with cowboy songs and two-steppers. Garth questioned whether the song was "country enough" to fit the collection. Reynolds pushed for it, and Garth decided to trust his producer's instincts.

Later, he would explain why he put so much faith in Reynolds, saying that he wished every artist had the pleasure of working with someone like him. "Allen is in it for the music and believes the music will speak for itself," Garth said. "I believe he's right. My biggest compliment was Allen Reynolds showing confidence in me. He is one of those special few."

"The Dance" eventually would be placed as the tenth and last song on Garth's first album. As Garth had perceived, it is unlike anything else on the debut, especially in musical content. Everything else on the album features fiddles, steel guitar, and acoustic interludes. "The Dance" opens with a dramatic piano introduction and glides along with a string section to provide a provocative, highly unusual setting for a country ballad.

Later, in a press release description of the song, Garth pinpointed "The Dance" with surprising honesty and foresight. "For me, this sums up the whole LP, my life, and my music. It's a great tune by my friend Tony Arata." It would be a year after the album's release before "The Dance" would begin receiving heavy radio airplay.

In 1990, after the success of "Friends in Low Places," he repeatedly expressed amazement that he had been blessed with two career songs at such an early point in his development. Then, in an interview a few hours prior to the *CMA Awards Show* on October 2, 1991, he remarked that "The Dance" had been the biggest song of his career so far. " 'Friends in Low Places' is definitely the highlight of my concerts, but 'The Dance' is something else, something very special," he said.

Garth cowrote the album's other emotionally stirring ballad, "If Tomorrow Never Comes," which became his first number-one song on the country singles chart. Garth got the idea one night, he has said, while "sitting up watching my wife sleep and wondering, 'If I died tomorrow, whether I had done my job and let her know how much I love her.' "

He passed the idea on to about one hundred different songwriters "who didn't find it worthwhile," according to Garth. Doyle then introduced him to Kent Blazy, who had written "Headin' for a Heartache," a hit for Gary Morris.

"We got together and worked on the song, which is partly about my wife, Sandy, and about his wife, Sharon. He basically wrote the bulk of it. I brought the beer."

In other interviews, however, Garth expands the definition of the song to give it broader meaning. "That song means a lot to me because of friends I've lost," Garth said, referring to his ex-roommate, Jim Kelley, who died in a car crash while the two were at Oklahoma State. "There's a million things you can say that need to be said."

The song was released, coincidentally, almost simultaneously with the movie *Ghost*, a box office smash starring Patrick Swayze and Demi Moore based on the same theme as Garth's song.

"Much Too Young (To Feel This Damn Old)" was in some ways a more conventional song, at least in its musical arrangement. Released a few weeks prior to the album, it indicated

*G*arth graduates Yukon High School, Yukon, Oklahoma, class of '80

*G*arth escorts Yukon High homecoming queen Jerry Castro.

*W*ith Yukon High head football coach Milt Bassett

RON WOLFSON / LONDON FEATURES

RON WOLFSON / LONDON FEATURES

LEE SALEM / SHOOTING STAR

*W*ith Perry O'Possum and the Judds, 1991

With Carl
Perkins

With Kitty
Wells and
Sandy

*G*arth and Sandy

*G*arth's parents,
Troyal and Colleen
Carroll Brooks

*W*ith Sandy, 1990

*A*t the Country Music Awards, 1991

Ropin' the Wind makes music history: number one on the pop and country charts. Jimmy Bowen of Capitol Records marks the event on September 24, 1991.

THE **Billboard** 20

THIS WEEK	LAST WEEK	2 WKS AGO	WKS ON CHART	ARTIST
				GARTH BROOKS CAPITOL NA
1	NEW		1	METALLICA ELEKTRA
2	1	1	5	NATALIE COLE ELEKTRA
3	2	2	14	COLOR ME BADD GIANT
4	5	4	8	BONNIE RAITT CAPITOL
5	4	3	12	BOYZ II MEN MOTOWN
6	6	5	18	C&C MUSIC FACTORY COLUMBIA
7	10	9	38	MICHAEL BOLTON COLUMBIA
8	9	8	21	R.E.M. WARNER BROS
		13	27	RUSH ATLANTIC
			2	

*S*ome 16,000 fans endure a heavy downpour at Fan Fair '91.

TOP ALBUMS

FOR WEEK ENDING
SEPTEMBER 28, 1991

TM	TITLE	PEAK POSITION
LE	ROPIN' THE WIND	1
	METALLICA	1
	UNFORGETTABLE	1
	C.M.B.	3
U	THE DRAW	2
N	HARMONY	3
O	DU SWEAT	2
N	NDERNESS	
	E TIME	
	ONE	

quickly that Garth's debut was going to receive strong recognition from radio, especially for a new artist.

The song was the first of several Garth has recorded about cowboys and rodeo competitors. In this one, he describes a veteran rodeo rider hustling down a highway to get to the next meet. He's tired of the road, tired of not getting enough rest, and tired of being away from his lover. She hasn't answered the phone at home for more than two weeks, so he suspects she's left him, and he wonders why she's stayed so long.

In interviews after the album's release, Garth has at times suggested that the song is about cocaine cowboys. But it works fine as a glimpse of the difficult life of a bronc rider, especially in the later stages of a tough, short career. "We never had any land or animals," said Garth, who also has admitted to a fear of horseback riding. "So I couldn't be a cowboy. But I can write and sing about 'em."

The first praise on "Much Too Young" came from reviewers in music trade magazines who try to tip radio programmers to good songs. *The Gavin Report*, a respected tip sheet for disc jockeys, said of the song: "What starts off as just another country tale of life on the road is made sublime by Brooks' expressive voice and the song's great hook. Seems this Tulsa native knows a thing or two about bronc riding, too. We're looking forward to hearing what else Garth has to offer."

Robert K. Oermann, a high-profile Nashville music critic, writes reviews of singles for *Music Row* magazine. He is read more for entertainment value by industry insiders than by radio executives. He, too, chimed in with positive remarks about Garth's debut song, saying: "By God country to the core. A hurtin' vocal, chiming steel, sawing fiddle and toe-tapping hillbilly beat. I don't care who else comes along in this listening session. I can tell you right now, just six records into the stack, that Garth Brooks has my heart as Discovery of the Day."

Billboard tends toward a more reserved style, yet the praise is evident in its listing of "Much Too Young" as a "Recommended" hit for country radio. "A dark but uptempo essay on the rigors of road-weariness and loneliness. Spirited, cry-in-the-voice treatment and moody, imaginative instrumentation."

When the song hit radio, the kudos really began pouring in, and Garth's comanager, Pam Lewis, exercised her publicity muscle to gather comments from disc jockeys at leading radio stations across the country in an attempt to convince other stations to join the party.

He had taken a big first step. His introduction would pick up even more speed with the release of "If Tomorrow Never Comes," which became his first number-one record.

As "Tomorrow" ran its course, Garth started to realize the power a national radio hit can have over listeners. A woman from Virginia wrote to say she had been contemplating suicide until hearing the song. "She said that ever since then, her life has been turned around," Garth told the Associated Press.

The Virginia woman was homeless and had a family, and she thought they might be better off with one less mouth to feed. "Then she heard my song just before Christmas and it changed her mind," she said. "Her letter says it isn't easy, they're still struggling—but at least they're struggling."

The understanding of his newly gained power had a strong effect on him. In his interviews, his feelings about songs and their messages began to show up more stridently in print.

"Your songs are your swords, your power," he said. "It's amazing the size of the sword you carry. I'm looking for beliefs that need to be stated in this day and time. I try to let people know they aren't working for nothing, that what they see when they close their eyes at night doesn't always have to be a dream."

In the same interview, he added, "The music has got to be real. Country music isn't 'My dad got run over at the truck wash right after my wife left me this morning.' The music is set in a manner that everybody can relate to, not just the guy driving the truck. It's very real and people are turning to it. It's not stereotyped anymore. I look for things the common man would say, such as the guy at Wal-Mart. Real people today are going to Wal-mart."

Garth's next hit, "Not Counting You," also climbed to number one. A snappy Texas two-stepper with a clever lyrical twist, Garth nonetheless openly criticized Capitol's decision to release the song to radio before songs he liked more, namely the ballads "Everytime That It Rains" and "The Dance."

At the time of the album release, Garth explained: "I wrote this for a woman. I didn't expect it to be on the LP. At first it sounded too swing, like George Strait. Now it's one of my favorite cuts on the LP. We ended up giving it a kind of rockabilly feel. Good opening tune, great for concerts."

The song is the only one on the album written by Garth without a cowriter, and he naturally would be expected to like it. But five months later, when it was gaining radio play,

Garth was outspoken in his lack of enthusiasm for the tune.

"Being able to stand up for three minutes in front of the nation is quite a gift," he said. "And I think it's very important that you say something. I love this country, but the downfall of the United States is that nobody makes stands. Everybody wants to be a fence-walker. If you have opinions and values, I definitely think you should try to express them. That's why I'm not that big of a fan of my own single right now ["Not Counting You"]. The record company figured it was time to release a dance song, but I like doing the ballads and the serious songs a lot more.

"Music is really for the heart and soul, yes, but it's also a teaching process, a healing process. I know whenever I'm depressed I still go into a room and put on an album by Dan Fogelberg or James Taylor. Sometimes they make me downright depressed for a while. But that's what music is for, to create emotion."

As Garth's songs and his album continued to climb the country charts, the producers of a pilot for a potential television show, through a stroke of luck, found themselves able to capitalize on Garth's growing recognition. A television production crew from Los Angeles came to Nashville to film a cheaply put together update of the old hit network series *Adam 12*. The TV movie, *Nashville Beat*, was based on the premise that the two partners had separately relocated to Nashville and were reunited in their fight against crime. The pilot would feature the same two stars, Kent McCord and Martin Milner, who appeared in the original.

Garth's comanager, Pam Lewis, asked him to perform at a cast party for the movie crew. She thought it might lead to a role in the movie, since the script called for a cowboy singer to perform during a scene and the part had not yet been cast.

Garth impressed the crowd, a mixture of Hollywood crew chiefs and Nashville-based crew workers. He more than lived up to their expectations, a large, rowdy fellow who went a little overboard in his show, and he sang better than most of these decidedly noncountry fans would have expected.

After the party he was told to visit the production office the following work day. "As soon as I walked in, a little old lady said, 'You'll do.' She didn't say hi or nothing, just, you'll do. That was it. I just walked straight back out."

Garth later saw the program, which aired

on The Nashville Network and was quickly forgotten. Still, a lot of young performers might brag about appearing in a television show, no matter how bad the program. Not Garth. "I got to admit," he said. "I was never a huge fan of those people, and I really didn't think the show would be that good. But I found myself sitting there watching it. And it wasn't. It was a baaaad movie."

Chapter

☆ 12 ☆

With two consecutive number ones under his hat, Garth Brooks had become an entity in country music. He also was finding himself suddenly identified as one of several new, young male vocalists who wore cowboy hats. "Hat acts," they were called, occasionally derisively by some, by others simply as a way of quickly describing a certain type of traditional country music stylist.

George Strait had set the mold. Though others had worn cowboy hats before him, the style had grown to be a rarity in Nashville in the 1970s. Strait came to the fashion choice naturally; he had been a genuine ranch hand before his nighttime pursuit of singing started earning him enough money to trade in the ropes and brands for more comfortable tools, like an acoustic guitar and a microphone.

And Strait's success seemed to start a new trend. By the mid-1980s, two of the top new country stars were wielding huge cowboy hats. Neither Dwight Yoakam nor Ricky Van Shelton had worn them before, but by the time they started taking photographs for album covers, the hats had become a permanent part of their daily wear.

For the latter two, the hats served to cover thinning domes rather than to emphasize the new country music fashion direction pointed out by Strait. But their success seemed tied to their hats. Like the music these men performed, hats harkened to an earlier, more rugged, more simplisitc era in America. These guys were real men. They were hunks with hats.

By the beginning of the 1990s, it was hard to find a guy singing country music who dared venture into the public eye without a ten-gallon topper. In October 1991, four of the five nominees for CMA Male Vocalist of the Year wore cowboy hats—the list being George Strait, Garth, Clint Black, and Alan Jackson (a Georgia native and former mechanic who would be much more comfortable in a ball cap than Western wear). Singer Vince Gill, the lone topless nominee, joked that he was the leading nonhat candidate.

Garth began fielding more questions about whether he was a country traditionalist or not; he started seeing more articles that tossed him into the category of "hat act."

Few artists like labels, no matter how accurate they may be, and Garth started to speak out against these descriptions.

"As much as I hate the label a hat puts on you, if you take it off nobody knows who you are," he told a reporter. "It's damned if I do, and damned if I don't. If I put it on, people call me George Strait or Clint Black. If I take it off, they don't know who I am."

Though some of his songs were traditional in musical style ("Not Counting You," "Cowboy Bill," "Nobody Gets Off in This Town"), others were not ("The Dance," "If Tomorrow Never Comes").

"I think the labels will wear off as time passes," he snapped to a reporter. "I don't like to be boxed in. I think the only thing that will be predicatable about Garth Brooks is that I like surprises. That's always been one of my secret weapons, that people don't know what to expect of me."

He also suggested that he had been conservative in the choice of material and arrangements for his first album, and that that would never be the case again. "I was scared to death to make any kind of mistake on the first one," he said.

With the release of "The Dance," however, Garth didn't have to debate about how different he was from other country singers. The hit song did his talking for him.

On May 24, 1990, Garth and Sandy went out shopping to celebrate their fourth anniversary. When they returned, they found a message on their answering machine telling them that the album, *Garth Brooks*, had been certified gold for selling more than a half-million copies.

It was more than a year after the release of the album, and it didn't happen until after the release of the fourth single, "The Dance." And it didn't matter. Country music measures success by album sales, and Garth had just won his first jackpot.

More amazingly, however, the album doubled its sales within a month. "The Dance" was sending people into record stores to buy an album. "Ever since that anniversary, everything's been going wonderfully," Garth noted. "Ever since then, it seems like I can fall off a ten-story building and land in a truck full of money."

The song became a favorite at funerals, as

might be expected, and Garth received loads of letters from people who said the album helped them conquer their grief. He also heard of an Arkansas boy whose suicide note said, "Play 'The Dance' for me."

Asked about the letter, Garth responded, "It really hurts. The song isn't about death. It's about life, about doing everything you can with the time that God gives you."

Those buying an album found a variety of riches beyond what they had heard on the radio. The most dramatic of his nonhit songs is "Everytime That It Rains," an unusually complex song about a romantic encounter between a traveler and a waitress at a roadside cafe. In interviews, he has suggested the story is based on a real-life incident. "I'm very happily married," he said. "That's something that happened before I got married. It's not all true. I don't know how to explain it without giving it away. Part is fantasy, but it's based on reality."

On the lighter side, the album's most entertaining song is "Nobody Gets Off in This Town," a double-entendre about the lack of things to do in a town where the one stop light is always green.

Garth has a special fondness for unusual writers and songs. Larry Bastian and Dewayne Blackwell, the writers of "Nobody Gets Off in

This Town," are atypical Nashville songsmiths: Bastian is a former park ranger who used to send his songs from a California mountain town before finally moving to Nashville in the mid-1980s; Blackwell is a veteran pop writer whose credits include "Mr. Blue," the 1959 hit for the Fleetwoods. Blackwell moved to Nashville in the late 1980s.

Both names show up frequently on Garth's albums, suggesting he tends to be loyal to writers he likes. Bastian also wrote or cowrote two other songs, "Cowboy Bill" and "I've Got a Good Thing Going," on Garth's debut album. He also had a hand in writing "Unanswered Prayers" and was the lone writer of "Rodeo," the first hit from Garth's third album, *Ropin' the Wind*. Blackwell, meanwhile, is cowriter of "Friends in Low Places," and Garth covered his "Mr. Blue" on the second album, *No Fences*.

Repeater Tony Arata placed a song, "The Same Old Story," on Garth's second disc and Pat Alger cowrote "The Thunder Rolls" and "Unanswered Prayers" from the second album and "What's She Doin' Now" from the third.

Garth is always generous when speaking of his contribution to songs he's written with Bastian, Alger, and several others. "It's a kind of joint venture," he quips. "The trick is to come into a writing session when it's about over and say, 'Hi, guys. What are you working on?' "

Having achieved platinum-selling success in a town filled with songwriters, Garth will never have problems finding a writing partner anytime soon.

Chapter

☆ 13 ☆

Jimmy Bowen is the president of the Nashville division of Capitol Records, the company that gave Garth Brooks his chance to
record his songs. Bowen has long encouraged
his reputation as a freethinker who went his
own way and didn't care much for the self-
congratulatory zeal that seems as much a part
of the entertainment industry as spotlights and
sequins.

Garth Brooks had released his first album
shortly before Bowen moved to Capitol Records
in 1989 to take over as president of its Nashville operations. Simply titled *Garth Brooks*—
"I would have titled it *Randy Travis*, but I
didn't think I could get away with it," Garth
once quipped—the album had been on the mar-

ket several months and had yet to accumulate the sales figures many had predicted for it.

Current albums often suffer when a change takes place in the front office of a record company. The corporation loses sight of the product on the street when concentrating on the inner operation. As Capitol began assessing its status with Bowen at the helm, some executives suggested that it would be more prudent to concentrate on Garth's next album rather than trying to improve sales on one that already had not done well. The theory was, let this one falter and put together a better marketing plan for the next.

Garth's managers, Bob Doyle and Pam Lewis, fought that idea. They perceived a growing interest in the first album. They believed it had never received the kind of attention and financial commitment often required to make an album a hit, and they felt the album contained hit singles that had not been given a chance at radio airplay.

Two different stories exist of what happened next. A source closely involved with Capitol Records at the time says Bowen didn't want to continue pushing the first album. The opinion he offered, according to the source, was that the production was shoddy and that no potential hits could be found from the existing songs.

Bowen thought the smartest move would be to focus on making a better second album, to produce the young artist himself, and to build a fortified marketing and advertising plan for it.

In this version of the story, Garth and his managers fiercely disagreed. They had seen the crowds react to the song "The Dance" when Garth performed it in concert. They knew it had a palpable, overwhelmingly positive affect on listeners. They wanted to put it out as a single. Garth had a vision for a video he thought would give the song an extra dimension.

Bowen reportedly was impressed with their boldness and willingness to put their necks on the line. He agreed to give "The Dance" a shot despite his reservations.

Bowen, however, tells the story differently. According to his version, Capitol had not planned to promote the first album further. When he came aboard, he said, he thought "The Dance" was a powerful song and reversed the previous decision. He backed Garth's desire to create a video for it (though almost everyone acknowledges that Garth fought over the size of the budget for the video and over the final edits with Bowen and the video director). He was responsible for backing the managers and the artist in going forward with "The Dance" as a single, he claimed, and it wouldn't have happened had he not joined Capitol.

When a Nashville executive familiar with the workings of Capitol heard Bowen's version, he reacted by saying, "That lying son-of-a-bitch!"

However it occurred, Bowen gloated proudly when Garth became Capitol's best-selling artist. When his third album, *Ropin' the Wind*, jumped to the top of the charts its first week out, Bowen crowed. "This is one of the best things that's ever happened to us, to see one of our people explode like this," he told Jay Orr of the Nashville *Banner*. "I got into this business in 1956, and this is the first time since Elvis Presley that I've seen a solo entertainer have this kind of impact. He's selling out everywhere."

The enthusiasm ran throughout the circle of power gathered tightly around the Oklahoma singer. Comanager Pam Lewis predicted glowingly that the record-setting ways of *Ropin' the Wind* had only begun with the fireworks set off by initial sales. "The projections are that he's going to continue to sell away," she boasted the week the album came out. "They're saying this album will sell ten million copies."

Chapter
☆ 14 ☆

Garth Brooks's success arrived at a time when country music already was feeling flush with renewed popularity. Still, despite better times, the enormity and swiftness of Garth's impact shocked the country music industry. Perhaps no one really expected that a country artist could actually become as popular as, say, M. C. Hammer or Paula Abdul. Nashville, at best, had been hoping for a slightly bigger piece of the popular music pie. They never expected that a brash, sentimental lug of a guy from Oklahoma could swagger in and grab such a large portion.

Country music sales had started edging upward in the late 1980s after a disastrous drop earlier in the decade. Randy Travis had been the first to send ripples through the complacent music offices. With a sound many leaders once considered too old-fashioned for modern listeners, Travis had turned the tide toward traditionalism by selling more than a million copies of his first album. He went on to sell more than eight million albums in four years, becoming the first consistent million-seller to arise in country music since the group Alabama six years earlier.

Travis's popularity had followed the slow yet steady gains of George Strait and Reba McEntire, both of whom had inched up the ladder of success while proudly acknowledging their preference for traditional country styles.

Strait and McEntire, along with newcomer Ricky Skaggs and longtime roots music advocate Emmylou Harris, became the torchbearers of what has become known as the new traditionalism. They rebelled against the trend toward a slickly produced, cosmopolitan country sound that gained favor in the 1970s and received a boost during the short-lived country boom that followed the movie *Urban Cowboy*.

By 1990, the country resurgence had gained speed. Following Travis, several new male singing stars emerge, all featuring a deep-toned vocal style, chiseled facial features, sleekly muscular frames, humble dispositions, and a clean-cut attitude that carried their looks as well as their lifestyles.

This new group of male country stars gained several tags, including "the new country hunks" and "the hat acts," the latter a sometimes derogatory term coined because several of them were rarely seen without the shadow of a wide-brimmed cowboy hat cutting across the smooth skin of their faces. The roll call of these new country stars includes Ricky Van Shelton, Alan Jackson, Clint Black, Mark Chesnutt, Joe Diffie, and Doug Stone, among others.

The group as a whole received buckets full of critical acclaim by journalists and country insiders for returning to a traditional sound that emphasizes fiddles, pedal steels, and two-stepping rhythms instead of string sections, synthesizers, and glossy sophistication.

It was an old sound spruced up by new technology and crisper recording techniques, and it drew a new audience while firing up loyal fans with renewed interest. In 1990 an unprecedented thirty-one country music albums achieved gold or platinum certification for selling more than five hundred thousand or one million copies respectively. The Nashville divisions of major record labels showed increased profits at a time when much of the record industry was struggling through a recession.

The Nashville community certainly took notice. "The audiences are definitely getting younger—and they're getting bigger," noted Stan Byrd, manager of Mark Chesnutt and Earl Thomas Conley, in a March 8, 1991, article in the trade magazine *Radio & Records*.

The audiences were turning out for established, traditional country music stars as well as for the newbloods. "There are young people at Merle Haggard, Conway Twitty, and George Jones shows that shouldn't be there," Byrd continued. But they were there, having a grand time and telling their friends.

The new stars, including Garth, reported singing autographs for diehard fans who wore T-shirts emblazoned with the logos of Metallica, AC/DC, Aerosmith, Cinderella, and other popular rock 'n' roll acts.

Tony Conway, the respected and experienced president of one of Nashville's oldest booking agencies, Buddy Lee Attractions, noticed the trend, too. He also had hard evidence. "The crowds are getting younger," he said. "I'm going on what I've personally seen and on the merchandisers' reports. And I'm seeing numbers I've never seen before, and faces I've never seen." The shift in the makeup of country music audiences, Conway suggested early in 1991, had changed dramatically within two years.

Stan Moress, an artist manager who works with K. T. Oslin and Lorrie Morgan, makes it a point to walk among the audiences at his artists' concerts. He reported similar findings: "The demographics are coming down. . . . I see an excitement that hasn't been there before."

The executives weren't the only people picking up on America's growing fondness for country music. Corporations and Madison Avenue advertisers began to hear a country beat. "We're getting interest out of national sponsors that wouldn't touch country a couple of years ago," Stan Byrd said. "The visibility of the format and the artist is higher than ever."

Country music leaders could come up with several reasons why country suddenly seemed cool to more people, especially to more younger listeners. "Young people have more input into the business," Moress said. "There are more young people at the record companies, at the trades, and in all aspects of the music business."

Byrd cited improvements at radio stations as playing a part. "Radio's presentation of country music has improved. The music is fresher, more appealing to a younger audience than that of other stations."

Other executives pointed to pop music for an explanation of the phenomenon. People were coming to country music because they were put off by the dance music, rap music, and hard rock that had come to dominate contemporary pop radio. In other words, it wasn't the quality of country that attracted new listeners; it was the lack of quality of its competition.

Still, country music, even with its growing popularity, continued to struggle with its long-standing inferiority complex. But something was stirring that no one seemed to understand. How could country increase and capitalize on this unusual new interest among the MTV generation? Who would lead the way? The question was asked often in Nashville, but the answer was evasive.

Chapter

☆ 15 ☆

Clint Black and Garth Brooks were born three days apart in February of 1962, Clint near Houston, Texas, and Garth in Tulsa, Oklahoma. Their debut albums came out on nearly the same day in April 1989. They both prefer striped shirts, Resistol hats, stone-washed jeans, and cowboy boots.

Clint Black's *Killin' Time* charged out of the blocks like a bronco at a Grand National Rodeo championship. The first single, "Better Man," went to number one. It sold a half-million copies in four months. *Killin' Time* became the number-one country music album in the United States. By January 1990, less than eight months after the unknown singer first surfaced, the album had sold a million copies.

It became the first debut album in country music to feature five number-one singles. It sat at the poll position of the country music album charts for more than thirty weeks. It remains the fastest-selling debut album in the history of country music, and it launched the most impressive first year of a performer in country music history.

Garth Brooks, in comparison, bucked out of the gate with a little less firepower with his first album. His initial single, "Much Too Young (To Feel This Damn Old)," reached a respectable number eight on the country music singles charts. His second, the tender "If Tomorrow Never Comes," reached number one. His sales topped the half million mark after eight months, an excellent response at any time in country music. Only this time it was overshadowed by the fireworks surrounding the broad smile of Mr. Black.

Moreover, because of their similarities in appearance and the parallel timing of their starts, Clint and Garth were locked into a competitive comparison game judged by how the numbers racked up.

The reasons behind why any act captures favor are as mysterious as to why someone chooses one person to date over another. But certain factors can help or hinder a career, especially in its early stages.

Clint Black worked with a high-powered, rock 'n' roll manager, Bill Ham, who teamed with ZZ Top to build their Texas blues-rock career; Garth Brooks hooked up with two new artist-managers, Bob Doyle and Pam Lewis, the former a veteran publishing industry executive with the performing rights society, ASCAP, and the latter a veteran publicity agent who had worked with MTV and RCA Records.

Clint Black recorded for RCA Records, at the time the most successful record company in Nashville, especially in establishing powerful new careers; Garth Brooks recorded for Capitol, which at the time had a poor track record in creating new acts or maintaining older ones. Ham and RCA invested heavily in setting Clint's career onto its meteoric course; Garth's managers were ground-level workers who waited for money to come in in order to reinvest it in their artist, and Capitol's pockets were relatively small, too.

The concurrent rising of their stars also created some confusion: One Texas reporter who interviewed Garth in 1989 called him "Garth Black" in the newpaper's headline, in the caption under the picture, and through the first half of the article. Mysteriously, the name changed to Garth Brooks in the second half of the story.

When he was first asked if a rivalry existed or if it was just a figment in the mind of the media, Garth answered with characteristic aw-shucks openness. "Shoot, no, man, that's not in anybody's mind, that's as real as life," he blurted to a reporter, laughing out loud and slapping his thigh. "We came out the exact same day, both wearing stripes and Stetsons. His 'Better Man' and my 'Much Too Young (To Feel This Damn Old)' had kind of the same tempo."

In another interview, he admitted the competition took on a friendly tone once the two had met. "I tried to hate him, 'cause I thought I should," he told Gary Graff of the *Detroit Free Press*. "But he and his band are very gracious, very nice people. And he likes James Taylor as much as I do, so how could I not like him?"

When a similar angle was pursued by yet another journalist, Garth suggested that the rivalry gave him a healthy incentive to push himself. "Clint and I are real competitive, no doubt about it. But I'd say we're also friends. We're hoping not so much to have the older stars' baton passed to us, but just to help keep the quality level respectable we want to maintain the standards our peers set."

The gleam that seems a permanent part of Garth's cornea surely was glowing fully as he continued: "But I've always loved sports, I'll tell you that. Without competition, you'll never get any better. That doesn't mean I don't yearn to be number one. It's like when you're in the race, you see the guy ahead of you keep plugging away, keep trying to eat up ground. The competition between Clint and me is the kind that keeps my blood boiling."

At other times, Garth seemed to weary of the comparisons. Perhaps the interview came at a moment when he was feeling worn down and tried of the grind of constant touring, the endless combination of shows, bus rides, hotel rooms, autograph signings, radio promotions, and telephone interviews. "If you want to know the truth, I have all the respect for [Clint] in the world. Unless I'm mistaken, he's a pretty sharp kid—and that's all he is, too, man. He's just a kid. They're throwing all this in his face, and he's handling it the best he can."

As time wore on, however, and Garth slowly started gaining momentum on his peer, the tone of his conversations about Clint Black shifted. More and more, he wanted to get away from discussing the competition and point out how he differed from the Texan.

"Clint and I are not in the same groove,"

Garth told Atlanta newspaper reporter Russ DeVault. A month later, his game plan started to become more apparent when he responded to the rivalry question by saying: "[Clint] is a stylist. From the very first two notes, he wants you to know that it's Clint Black. And me, I want people to sit there and say, 'What the hell is this? What's going on here?' "

In other words, Garth seemed to have heard the criticism that too much of the new country singers were starting to sound alike, even look alike. One critic, writing about Garth, referred to him as "a calculating fake . . . a clone of George Strait."

Within a year of his first record release, he purposefully went about altering the perception that he was another traditionalist singer only interested in following the footsteps of George Jones, Merle Haggard, and George Strait. Garth started to position himself in a different light.

Instead of paying homage only to country music legends, Garth began prominently dropping the names of other important influences. He'd say that he yearned for recognition as a writer, a singer, and a live performer, then add, "That's why I love a guy like Billy Joel—he does all three phenomenally." His shows were peppered with covers of familiar pop songs, including those by Don McLean ("American Pie";

"Vincent"), Elton John ("Rocket Man"), Dave Loggins ("Please Come to Boston"), the Georgia Satellites ("Keep Your Hands to Yourself"), as well as oldies by George Jones.

However, Garth hailed two older artists more than any others. In some instances, he'd say James Taylor was his favorite singer-songwriter. At other times, it would be Dan Fogelberg.

At some point he decided to start emphasizing these gentler influences over the hard-bitten ones. "If I'm sensitive or it comes out in my music, that's a compliment. It's just another form of surprise for me. That's probably the greatest weapon I've ever had all of my life—in sports and everything—was surprise. I have a thousand more directions to go in. That's simply because I've always been a kid at heart. And, as a kid, I always liked to dress up and play somebody that I wasn't."

By the end of 1990 his list of influences had stepped deeper into pop music and further from country standbys. "I'm a huge fan of the commercial late seventies rockers: Boston, Journey, REO Speedwagon, Fleetwood Mac, Steve Miller," he told *Entertainment Weekly*.

In addition, his concerts grew increasingly loud and raucous, with the singer charging about the stage like a linebacker with rhythm, climbing rope ladders, jumping on speakers, smashing guitars, and throwing water onto crowds.

His desire to differentiate himself from his colleagues became more apparent when his clothes started to grow more outrageous. In private, Garth prefers comfortable athletic wear, lounging his few quiet days away in sweat pants, T-shirts or sweatshirts, gym shoes and maybe a ball cap. In public, however, his fashion sense flew to the outer galaxy of rodeo cowboy wear: black shirts with shoulders blaring in neon sea green or shirts with outrageously bold-colored stripes.

He began sneaking John Wayne into conversations whenever the opportunity was presented. When a fan magazine reporter asked him if a movie was to be made on his life, which movie star would he like to see take the lead role, Garth replied, "John Wayne," and spoke of Wayne in the present tense as he described him as a prototypical American who represented everything that the singer aspired to be, to stand for, and to accomplish.

In another instance, Garth said of Big John: "I'd like to carry the same messages in song that he did in his movies. He stood for honesty."

Garth also became more outspoken on political and social topics as he picked up more experience with the press, though his topics tended toward the safest areas possible. Like most conservatives, Garth huffed and puffed about the idea of someone burning the American flag, and he started speaking more flamboyantly about patriotism and his love for the good ol' U.S. of A. Criticizing those who burned flags was hardly a controversial issue to those whom Garth was likely to appeal or to the middle Americans who Garth felt he represented. Nonetheless, it's the type of action few country stars dare take, instead avoiding politics as aggressively as they might dismiss an instrumentalist who came to an audition with a mohawk haircut.

Early in 1990, when Garth's strident campaign to distance himself from his peers was in full swing, a radio interviewer asked him which country he would like to visit. "The United States of America," he said without irony, no doubt filling his chest with air and throwing his shoulders back. Asked if he would sign up to fight if the United States went to war, he replied: "As quick as I could get down there, yes, ma'am."

His own words must have surprised him. He backpedaled: "I'll take my stand, and if it takes dying for that stand, that's what I'll do. I mean, that's the way I feel now. If the situation comes up I might run like hell, but right now I feel that way."

When America did declare war a year later, Garth apparently reconsidered his passion for enlisting for the service. (Comanager Bob Doyle, however, a member of the Air Force reserves, was called to duty as a pilot and spent several weeks in Saudi Arabia.)

On flag-burning, when a South Bend, Indiana, radio station asked Garth to make an appearance at a specially planned protest against flag-burners and in support of a flag-burning amendment, Garth suggested that he commit himself further and perform in a fund-raising benefit. The station quickly set up the show.

"We've done some free shows in support of the flag-burning," Garth told reporter Sandy Lovejoy. When she asked him if he understood what he had said, he acted horrified and hurried to correct himself. "No, ma'am. I think anybody that talks to me for more than three or four seconds knows I wouldn't be for that."

It's hard to judge whether Garth's bolder personality, performances, and appearance were calculated to set him apart from the pack of young country stars or was simply a man feeling more comfortable with himself and his public persona and therefore more freely expressing his individuality. Whichever, one point was evident: Garth was becoming zealous in his desire to cut his own path, and he was attempting to establish an identity in every way possible.

By the fall of 1990 the strategy was working. "Garth Brooks Certainly Not Ordinary" read a headline in a Wisconsin newspaper. "Garth Brooks Shuns Any Categorization" claimed another in Texas. He no longer belonged to the crowd of faceless guys in hats who sing country music.

Chapter

☆ 16 ☆

With the release of *No Fences*, Garth might as well have thrown his hat to the wind. He no longer would be burdened with descriptions of being a hat act, a George Strait clone, or a traditional music revivalist.

He was clearly attempting to create something more unique and individual, an admirable artistic decision that usually results in country artists struggling with critical acclaim but little airplay or sales. But Garth managed to progress, to take risks, and to attract a larger audience simultaneously. He managed to strike a chord in the American heartland with a sound and style distinctively his own. It's the stuff of all legends and quite likely the beginning of a long, significant career.

The album caught on immediately, too. In fact, it caught on faster than he wanted.

A radio executive in Oklahoma City who had been an early supporter of Garth's records had, over the previous year, established a rapport with the singer and his family. When word of an upcoming album spread through an eager radio community, the executive contacted Colleen Carroll Brooks and asked her about it. She excitedly told him about the fresh sound Garth had created and that the first song was a fantastic, catchy singalong everyone would enjoy.

He asked if he could get a copy; she agreed to bring one by. Whether she told him he couldn't play it has been disputed, but it also is an empty argument on his behalf. Any radio programmer knows it's considered a major sin to play the first single from an album prior to its official release date.

Radio people, competitive as they are, love a scoop. This one was achieved by tricking a performer's mother. Adding to the damage, the executive made copies of the song and sent them to stations affiliated with his own. All of a sudden, a select handful of radio stations were playing Garth's new song, "Friends in Low Places," and receiving a wildly popular response.

To make matters worse, of course, the competing stations were receiving requests for a song they didn't have yet. Stations across America besieged Capitol Records demanding a copy from Capitol, and the company was forced into releasing the song weeks ahead of schedule. The result was a hit song climbing a chart, but fans wouldn't be able to buy the album for several more weeks. All of the careful planning set up around a major record release had been thrown off by one radio executive.

"Mom was just doing what she thought would help her son," Garth said. "They took advantage of her."

Jimmy Bowen, as president of Garth's record company, simply took it as an example of his star's amazing standing in the music community. "Leaks like his happened to me when I worked in pop music, but never in my career in country music have we had a situation like this," Bowen reported. "I know this kid is hot, but this is amazing."

With *No Fences*, Garth's sales initially took place in the Southwest, especially Texas and Oklahoma, the same region that accounted for more than 50 percent of the sales of the first album. But, before long, the numbers spread across the United States.

Garth first heard the song "Friends in Low Places" when he sang it in early 1989 on a demo for the songwriters Dewayne Blackwell and Earl Bud Lee, who then planned to use Garth's version to pitch it to other artists. At the time, Garth was an unknown entity: He had already completed his first album, but no one outside his circle of advisers had heard it. Garth loved "Friends in Low Places" immediately, and he wanted it for his second album. He kept in touch with the writers for months afterward, constantly checking to see if anyone else had asked to record it. He kept telling them he wanted it for himself.

When Garth started work on *No Fences*, however, he didn't record "Friends in Low Places" right away. Blackwell panicked, thinking he had lost a cut, so he started pitching it to other producers. Mark Chesnutt, another new artist, quickly recorded it.

When the news got back to Garth, "I went through the roof," he said. "It scared me to death. I called them up and finally got a note in writing that I had the license for it. I believe in fighting for what I believe is mine. I followed the rules, and it was my song."

Indeed, it was. But by the time Blackwell approved the rights for Garth to record the song—a move that surely drew a strong negative reaction from Mark Chestnutt and his record company—the Oklahoma singer had also agreed to record "Mr. Blue," another Blackwell song.

Approving the licensing for a cut of a song after giving it to another singer is against the unwritten laws of the Nashville music industry. Both Garth and Chestnutt, however, claim they were wronged by Blackwell. But Garth released the single first, and his version is the one people will be singing for decades to come. Meanwhile, Blackwell receives royalty payments for two songs from the astronomical sale of *No Fences*.

The album continued to keep pace with the sales levels initiated by the success of the rowdy first song. Other hits continued to show off Garth's range, from the ballads "Unanswered Prayers" and "Victim of the Game" to the high-stepping "Two Of a Kind," and "Working On a Full House" to the issue-oriented song about adultery, "The Thunder Rolls."

No Fences launched Brooks on his record-setting ways. The album sold more than 700,000 copies in the first ten days of its release, and it achieved a higher ranking on the pop album charts than any country album in five years.

Chapter

☆ 17 ☆

Garth's move toward truly conquering America began shortly before the Country Music Association Awards show in the fall of 1990. Considered the most sought-after honors within the country industry, the gala is a good monitor of who's on top and who's not in country music. When the nominees were announced the preceding August, the lineup indicated how strongly Garth had barged his way to the front. To the surprise of nearly everyone, Garth Brooks became that year's leading nominee, ahead of Travis, Strait, Shelton, McEntire and, most notably, ahead of Black.

That same month he attracted more than nine thousand fans to a free concert at Forest Park Band Shell in the unlikely country music outpost of Queens, New York.

On October 4, 1990, his debut album was declared platinum for selling more than one million copies. Three days later, his second album, *No Fences*, crossed the same milestone less than three months after its release. The same weekend, he was named the sixty-fifth member of the Grand Ole Opry during the Opry's sixty-fifth birthday celebration. (He became the Opry's youngest member, but not the youngest person ever inducted. Hank Williams, for one, had already been kicked off the Opry and had died by the age of 28, Garth's age at the time he joined.)

That same week, the Country Music Hall of Fame and Museum requested that Garth donate his trademark hat and striped shirt for posterity and safekeeping. And his hometown of Yukon, Oklahoma, announced that it was gong to emblazon his name on a water tower to go along with the signs leading into town, which read, "Yukon, Home of Garth Brooks."

Garth's CMA Awards nominations were for Male Vocalist of the Year, Single of the Year, and Song of the Year for "If Tomorrow Never Comes"; Horizon Award (for best new artist); and Video of the Year Award for "The Dance." The night of the show Brooks sat prominently in the third row with his wife, Sandy. His parents, Troyal Brooks and Colleen Carroll Brooks, proudly sat further back.

In an interview a few days prior to the glittery awards event, Garth downplayed the importance of sweeping the show. "I got this one covered," he quipped. "And you're gonna say, 'What a cheesy way out of this thing.' But, right now, if somebody shot me, they'd take me into the hospital and I'd find out that the bullet was a collector's item worth two million bucks or something. I mean, things are going so well for me right now, I gotta go into that night knowing that if I walk away with zero or five or anything in between, it's the best thing that could happen to me. And just because you win doesn't mean you're the best."

Garth learned quickly that he wasn't going to enjoy a major sweep. The star-studded affair is traditionally all sequins, black ties, tuxes, bright lights, and cameras. Held at the comfortable Grand Ole Opry House, which holds 4,400 people who pay at least one hundred dollars a ticket, the CMA Awards show is telecast live nationwide by CBS and is seen in more than eighty other countries. It's country music's version of the Grammys, the Emmys, and the Oscars, and the night is rich in glamour and high anxiety.

On October 8, 1990, the awards presentations opened with Vince Gill's surprise win of Single of the Year for "When I Call Your Name." Before long, the Song of the Year award went to Jon Vezner and Don Henry, who had written "Where've You Been" for Kathy Mattea. Then Clint Black picked up the Male Vocalist of the Year honor. Garth and Sandy had plenty of time to sit and watch the show, and Garth was the first to leap to his feet and lead the crowd in a standing ovation when George Jones walked out on stage to perform a duet with Randy Travis.

The video award came late in the program, and the producers already had decided to try to hurry up the late-running program by skipping the part where the winner comes up to accept the honor. Instead, it would simply be announced with little fanfare. When "The Dance" was named, the cameras panned quickly to Garth as he gazed at Sandy and whispered something to her. He wasn't proclaiming his desire to stand on stage and accept an award for a video he had fought over with his record company and its director. What he said was, "All right, that's the one I wanted." He had pushed for a certain creative vision, and he had won—the battle *and* the award.

Later, though, he reacted with much more visible jubilation when named winner of the Horizon Award. After a long pause and an intense embrace with Sandy, Garth headed for the stage. A few steps away, though, he stopped, returned to his wife, and grabbed her hand.

"Come with me," he urged. She resisted, and he pulled and pleaded again. She smiled broadly and nervously as she grabbed his hand and walked the stairs alongside him.

His first words upon reaching the stage were about the woman he pulled along with him. "I'm not much good at it, but when I don't sing, I try and be a husband. This is my wife, Sandy." But it was his final comment that drew press attention afterward and which promoted his reputation as a controversial rising star: "I want to thank the good Lord because He's done a hell of a lot for me," he crowed.

Later, in an interview with writer Bob Millard, Brooks explained his need to have Sandy beside him. "We'd been holding hands all night, and to tell you the truth, it seemed more unusual to leave her than to take her with me. She was very excited." He also was glad he had her with him because she helped him regain his composure once he reached the platform. "Only two times in my life have I ever stood before a microphone and not had anything to say—and they both happened to me in the same week," he recalled with a chuckle.

As for his closing statement, which some

members of the Bible Belt might consider blasphemous, Brooks apologized for it as soon as he reached the backstage press corps. "I didn't mean to say that," he immediately said.

Later, he admitted that his friends got a kick out of it, but he still wished he's chosen other words. "I had to take a lot of kidding about that acceptance speech," he noted. "After I made the statement, I told myself, 'I can't believe the statement I just made.' One songwriter friend of mine came up to me later and joked, 'Oh, God, that Garth Brooks is a helluva guy.'"

During the CMA show, Garth also performed a highly animated version of his hit "Friends in Low Places," the extremely popular number one song that had been the initial song release to radio from his second album, *No Fences*.

Garth Brooks victories that week loomed much larger than they appear on paper. He won only two of the five awards he was nominated for, and the Horizon and Video awards are slightly less significant than being named the year's top male vocalist or taking home the trophy for the year's best song or best single.

But his performance ranked with Mary Chapin-Carpenter's hilarious ditty about being an opening act for other stars as the most talked about event of the telecast. Bringing his wife on stage with him was widely heralded as the most endearing, spontaneous action while accepting an award to occur during the CMA affair in several years. Combined with the Opry induction, the Hall of Fame presentation, his platinum album achievements, this recognition brought him to another important level of national stature.

"Garth Brooks made his move last week in his yearlong horse race with Clint Black," said a lead story in *USA Today*. "Garth Brooks mentally upstages CMA rivals," blurbed another news headline.

He also seemed to understand the score. Despite his losses he said that he was thrilled to be there and to win anything at all. "When they said my name," he would later say, "it was like I was a kid back in school and I thought I was in trouble."

He went on to touch upon a point rarely mentioned by country artists; that awards can knock the wind out of performers just as quickly as they can fill their sails. "Charlie Louvin [a veteran of the Louvin Brothers and a Grand Ole Opry performer] said awards were made to break people's hearts," Brooks said after the show. "Awards are like numbers on the charts. When they're working for you, they mean the world. When they're not, they're breaking your heart."

But perhaps the most interesting post-awards comment he made concerned his larger view of his career. "I want to stay hungry," he said, referring to the fact that he keeps his awards in the back of a bedroom closet. "I don't want to be satisfied with what I've done." Consequently, he chooses not to see his awards each morning as he starts his day.

The week following the show, Garth's *No Fences* album sold more than three hundred thousand copies. For the rest of September 1990, it average about two hundred and twenty-five thousand in weekly sales. It leaped to the top of the country album charts, finally toppling the Clint Black disc. More amazingly, it made number twelve on the pop album charts, becoming the highest charting country album since Dolly Parton joined forces with Emmylou Harris and Linda Ronstadt for the *Trio* album four years earlier.

In November, Macy's invited Garth to take a top star slot during its annual Thanksgiving Day parade, which is telecast across the nation on network television. "I'm on the turkey float," he said later. "Is that good?" Yes, since it allowed him to perform a new song, "Two of a Kind, Working on a Full House," to a national TV audience on a highly rated program.

In late December, the *Los Angeles Times*, in a year-end poll of the country music industry, asked twenty leading executives to predict which current artist would likely sell the most records over the next seven years. The poll gave ten points for every first-place finish, nine for second place, and so on. Garth topped the poll, receiving 166 points from mentions on 19 of the ballots. Clint Black came in second, garnering 164 points from 19 ballots. George Strait was a distant third, with 116 points.

"In many ways, we're talking one and one-A in terms of potential when we talk about Brooks and Black," one poll respondent said. "To me, Clint is a little sexier, feistier—a little mischievious. Garth is more down-to-earth, like the Rock of Gibraltar. He looks as honest as the day is long. Who's going to sell the most? It depends on who'll come up with the best material."

Others polled by reporter Robert Hilburn for the *Los Angeles Times* commented:

"The first thing you have to understand about Garth is, he's a tremendous entertainer. He's got showmanship, which you don't see a lot down here. And he'll stick around until four thirty in the morning signing autographs."

"Brooks isn't just an incredible singer. He also has something to say . . . a point of view that people outside of country music can identify with, whereas Clint and some of the others seem to sell mainly to a traditional country audience."

"He's influenced by Merle Haggard and Lefty Frizzell, but there's also a pop influence in there somewhere, and that may give him a wider audience."

"Seems like a pretty stubborn fella, which I like. He's willing to stretch out there a little bit, which means he'll keep growing as an artist."

Black also received some strong praise:

"Don't underestimate the charisma and the looks. He's sexy—not in the self-conscious way of Dwight Yoakam—but in the style of Johnny Cash or early Merle Haggard."

"He has the ability to sing in a bluesy, funky way, which gives him the potential to cross over into the pop field without losing his country touch or following."

But Black also received some less-than-positive comments. "To me, Black is already wearing a little thin, and I don't know if he's a good enough writer to keep that momentum going. That can be a big problem if he decides to just do his own material rather than turn to outside writers."

Early in 1990, Garth Brooks unabashedly boasted to a reporter, "I want to be the Artist of the Decade. I don't think there's anything wrong with setting your goals high. I think everyone should stride to be the best they can. I would be disappointed in myself if I aimed at becoming anything less than the best."

By December 31 of that year, Garth Brooks clearly had put himself on a path toward his goal. He had sold more than 2.5 million records in four months. His *No Fences* album remained at the top of the country music charts, and it would stay planted there until he released another album.

Chapter

☆ 18 ☆

Before Garth Brooks, about the only controversial aspect of country music videos was why the genre took so long to create clips on the level of quality as those in pop and rock music.

Garth, however, showed them that a bit of controversy can be good for business.

From the start, Garth didn't use video in the same way as other country music artists. With few exceptions, most country clips either followed low-budget, silly story lines or caught the artist in action.

The quality had been improving quickly in the late 1980s, however. Garth seemed determined not to create a cheap work simply for promotion. He repeatedly said he would put out videos only if they interpreted the songs in a significantly challenging way.

"I don't like to do videos because it robs the listener of their imagination," he said. "If I do one, it's to add a third dimension, something from out of left field."

His first clip, of "If Tomorrow Never Comes," changes the song's implied characters. In the song, the words suggest a conversation between a man and his wife. In the video, the images present a father speaking to his daughter.

"The Dance," which followed, was an ambitious clip that also added new meaning to the images suggested by the lyrics. Garth fought with the video director and his record company to have the video adhere to his vision. He demanded several edits, each causing Capitol to dip further into the bank.

The video combined footage of Garth performing the song in a starkly lit room with clips of John F. Kennedy, Martin Luther King, John Wayne, the late country singer Keith Whitley, and the late rodeo champion Lane Frost. It won several awards, including the Country Music Association's Video of the Year award in 1990.

Then, after shooting and paying for a video for "Friends in Low Places," Garth refused to allow his record company or his managers to release it. He didn't think it complimented the song, and he said he'd rather absorb the cost than put out something he didn't like.

Part of it showed up later in a video compilation of the singer's work, but even then he openly attacked the medium. "Right off the bat I'll tell you I'm not a big fan of videos, and I never have been," he said in interview footage on the tape.

He also joked about why he disliked watching his own videos. "TV has never been something that comes naturally to me," he said. "Whenever I see myself on TV, still to this day, I throw things at the TV. I think whenever you see yourself on TV, it's not how you see yourself in real life. I swear to you I don't have these double chins, and I have more hair than this right here," taking off his cowboy hat to point to his thinning skull. "I swear to you I do, but on TV it never seems to show up."

Then came "The Thunder Rolls," the first video by a major artist to be banned by the two leading country video presenters, Country Music Television and The Nashville Network, both owned by Gaylord Communications.

The video stepped beyond the story of adultery presented in the lyrics. The song's lyrics intimate that a wife may take violent action against her philandering husband. The video graphically illustrates the violence, as well as adding signs that the wife has been battered. In the video, the wife is beaten again by the man as he arrives home shortly before dawn. When the man heads toward his daughter in a threatening manner, the wife takes out a handgun and shoots him.

The day CMT decided to yank the video, after a few days of airing it, the station's general manager, Bob Baker, said the move was made because the clip "doesn't parallel the song" and that the violence was "gratuitous." He cited viewer complaints as playing a role in the final decision.

The director, Bud Schaetzle, spoke out against the banning immediately. "We think there's an intelligent viewing audience out there that understands such situations sadly do occur—and the video tries to raise that awareness."

The next day, TNN announced it would not air the video. "The violence is so strong and so graphic that it leaves you with a helpless feeling," said Paul Corbin, TNN program director. The station asked Garth to record a statement that could be tagged onto the video offering an 800 number where assistance can be provided for victims of domestic violence. Garth recorded the statement, then asked the station not to use it.

Within weeks, VH-1, a cable channel geared toward adult music listeners, announced that it would air the banned video.

Garth addressed the controversy in diplomatic terms at first, but later admitted feelings of anger. "Real life has brought me here," Garth later said in a prepared statement. "This video is a side of real life I guess people don't really want to see. I refuse to do a video that is just ordinary. It wastes the viewer's time and mine and my label's money. . . . The video has already done in two days what I hoped it would do in its lifetime . . . making people aware of a situation which unfortunately exists in our society and causing them to discuss it, sometimes even heatedly."

Months later, he told of having deeper feelings about the banning than he originally let on—even beyond the anger. "It crushed me," he told reporter Rob Tannenbaum. "I was shocked. I was so hurt. To go out there and do the makeup every morning for four hours . . . instead of just throwing some paint up on a sheet and dancing around—and then to get cut off by someone in the middle was just a big crock."

He then stated he had no desire to create another video, at least not for several years.

However, prior to the video's release, Brooks predicted the video would send out shock waves. "Believe me, man, this one takes it far out of what the words say," he told Nashville music journalist Jay Orr. "When it was over, it was like, 'Oh my God, what have I done?' "

Meanwhile, a video compilation featuring "The Thunder Rolls" and Garth's two other clips was hurriedly issued on a compilation for a list price of $14.99.

On October 2, 1991, the controversy reared again when the members of the Country Music Association voted "The Thunder Rolls" Video of the Year. When Schaetzle picked up his award for directing the video, he said to an audience on national television, "I hope everybody at TNN knows how much we appreciate your help."

Garth was backstage changing clothes from a performance a few minutes earlier, and later wondered why the video was presented at a different time than listed in his schedule. Nevertheless, he distanced himself from the director's on-stage remarks.

"The remark does not stand for Garth Brooks and his corporation," the singer said pointedly. "I love the people at The Nashville Network. Although my discontent and displeasure with them was very obvious, out of respect I never voiced my opinion."

When he accepted his award for Entertainer of the Year at the end of the celebration, he revealed how Sandy had objected angrily to the video's final cut. Before it was shot, but after a script had been circulated, Sandy asked Garth not to take part in a love scene and not to act as if he was going to strike the child. The video included both scenes.

But when the controversy hit, Garth told the CMA crowd, Sandy stood beside him, consoling and supporting him. "I haven't done anything to deserve this woman," he said, "but I wouldn't be here without her love and support."

Chapter

☆ **19** ☆

The new year, 1991, found Garth Brooks's star still on the rise.

His touring schedule slowed to ten dates in January and February only because he wanted it that way, and those dates were wildly successful. The *No Fences* album continued to sell at a remarkable clip. As his record company repeatedly exulted in press materials, "The Garth Brooks phenomenon keeps growing on a daily basis."

Radio & Records and *Billboard* magazines both crowned Brooks Male Artist of the Year and cited "The Dance" as the most performed song of the year. His single "If Tomorrow Never Comes" was tapped as the year's best song by the Nashville Songwriters Association International, the American Music Awards, and Britain's *Country Music People* magazine. The National Association of Record Merchandisers joined the fun, honoring him as the year's best-selling male country vocalist.

By March the honor roll was just beginning to unfurl. The readers of *Radio & Records* magazine, mostly country radio disc jockeys and program directors, gave Brooks every award in every category in which he qualified: Performer of the Year, Best Male Vocalist, Best Single ("Friends in Low Places"), Best Album (*No Fences*).

In announcing this massive sweep, *R & R* cited some of Brooks's accomplishments, including four number one records in 1990: "Not Counting You," "The Dance," "Friends in Low Places," and "Unanswered Prayers." Altogether, those records occupied the top spot on the singles chart for a total of nine weeks, more than any other country artist that year. (At the time, "No Fences" had sold more than 2.7 million copies, and the debut album had sold over a million.)

Garth handled the success just as he had gained it, with a blend of bravado and gee-whiz modesty. "I'm getting to do what I love and getting paid damn good for it," he told *People* magazine. At the same time, he would turn around and tell a newspaper columnist, "Believe me, man, it's got nothing to do with how talented you are. There's millions of people [in Nashville] that are ten times more talented than I am. It's just getting your break."

Asked about the advantages of stardom by the *Los Angeles Times*, Garth turned more Jimmy Stewart than John Wayne. "It's a lot easier to cash my checks at the grocery store now," he responded. "But as far as being a star, that's pretty much a four-letter word in my book. I'm just a guy who plays country music and happens to love what he does."

In April 1991, his coronation as country music's brightest star of the year was secured at the Academy of Country Music annual awards show. The Academy, a Southern California–based trade agency, exists primarily to make a large amount of money during the gala, which blends country artists with television personalities and promotions for Universal Studios.

Garth took home an unprecedented six awards: Entertainer of the Year and best single, song, album, video, and male vocalist. The previous biggest single-night wins had occurred when Mickey Gilley won five awards in 1977 and Freddie Hart accepted a similar quintet in 1972.

"I'm happy, but I'm a little embarrassed," Garth said when besting George Strait, among others, in the vocalist category. "I just want Mr. Strait to know he's always my male vocalist [of the year]."

Garth's biggest surprise of the night, and his biggest coup, was winning the prestigious Entertainer of the Year award so early in his career. When he accepted the final trophy, he simply tipped his hat and said, "I'm having a ball. Thank you all."

Backstage, as at the podium, Garth spoke with uncharacteristic contriteness, acting genuinely stunned by his overpowering sweep of the night's honors. "I hired the right people," he said softly as reporters prodded him to explain his amazing triumph.

To give some perspective as to how quickly Garth had zoomed to the top of his profession, consider this: His first album came out rather quietly exactly two years to the month before the ACM Awards; a year earlier, he still had not sold five hundred thousand albums. In the last year, then, more than four million albums had been sold. The six awards only added to the attention galloping in his direction.

Amid this hurricane of honors, the day Garth will never forget came on stage at the annual Fan Fair gathering at the Tennessee State

Fairgrounds in Nashville. For country music, Fan Fair is the big June swoon: More than twenty thousand tenaciously fervent fans pay a sixty-dollar fee for the right to enjoy four days of intense, all-day autograph sessions and several all-star shows. The fair brings more than seven million people annually to Nashville and has attracted more than three hundred thousand since its beginning in 1972.

Fan Fair was originally created simply to relieve the congested crowds that flock to Nashville each October for Country Music Week, which centers around the CMA Awards Show, the Grand Ole Opry birthday celebration, a convention of concert promoters and booking agents, a Grand Master Fiddlers Convention, and several banquets honoring songwriters and country music veterans.

Because such activities draw most of country music's biggest stars, the fans naturally gravitate to the city in hopes of glimpsing their favorite artists.

Fan Fair, as its name implies, gives the fans their own week. The first Fan Fair attracted about five thousand fans and presented more than one hundred artists in over twenty hours of entertainment. But no description can match the colorful frenzy of watching the most star-crazed autograph and snapshot seekers in mankind swarm after their favorite performers. The artists set up in some 450 booths crammed bumper-to-bumper in five gigantic corrugated steel and concrete buildings. Temperatures never fail to climb toward the 100-degree mark. Robert K. Oermann, veteran music reporter for the daily *Tennessean*, has aptly described it as a "crazed fiesta of the proleteriat."

By 1991, with country cranking out new stars with a heightened hunk factor, the Fan Fair had suddenly grown younger, giving the scene an electrical charge of expectation. The star they most eagerly yearned to see was Garth Brooks.

Dressed in a loud black-and-purple striped shirt and black denim pants, Garth met a blinding flash of Instamatic bulbs as he entered the Fan Fair stage, situated in the center of a race car track. In the grandstands and makeshift chairs in front of the stage, some sixteen thousand fans screamed and leapt to their feet despite a steady downpour of rain.

Two songs into his performance, Garth was interrupted by the imperious Jimmy Bowen. As president of Capitol Records, he announced to the gathering, he had come to honor his most cherished moneymaker. Bowen came bearing heavy metal: a platinum album mounted into a glassed frame. The black ink engraved into the silver plaque below the disc says that this honor is given to Garth Brooks to commemorate sales in excess of one million copies of the Capitol Records cassette and compact disc of his debut album, *Garth Brooks*. A double-platinum award followed for the same one.

The next one was gold, honoring five hundred thousand units sold for "No Fences." Then Bowen presented a platinum award for the second album, then a double-platinum. Garth was smiling, shaking his head, and generally holding himself with humble dignity. That changed when George Jones, the most revered singer of the new generation of country stars, stepped from a hidden corner of the backstage area carrying an award signifying triple platinum, or more than three million sales.

Garth's face blanched with emotion as he recognized the king of honky-tonk music. Two years earlier, just as his debut album was released, a Georgia newspaper writer had asked Garth what honor he most desired in country music. "Anything presented to me by George Jones," he had replied.

As Jones walked toward him, Garth yanked the cowboy hat from his head and positioned it over his heart. As Jones started to talk into the microphone, Garth visibly sobbed. When Sandy proudly carried yet another plaque, this one signifying four million in sales, her husband openly bawled.

"The rain had a lot to do with my emotions," the singer told journalist Rob Tannenbaum later that day, "because it stood for the fact that the people that believe in this organization are not fair-weather people. They sit in the rain, they sit in the heat."

That, and the fact that his dream of receiving an honor by his favorite country singer had come true so early in his life. "The first time I met George Jones," Brooks recalled, "I cried. When I shook his hand, the tears kept popping out of my face. I felt real wimpy, but boy, I'll never forget that. That's a side I wish I could control more, the tender side. 'Cause it makes you feel like a big puss when you break down in front of twenty thousand people. I'd like to be cooler than that."

But it's tenderness that plays as much a role in his popularity as his rowdier tendencies. It's the balance between the cocky reveler in "Friends in Low Places" and the sentimentalist whose voice breaks gently in "If Tomorrow Never Comes" and "The Dance" that has attracted crowds willing to withstand a torrential rain just to see him perform and hear him sing.

Later the same day, he pushed through one of the exhibition halls. Though led by a police escort, the scene wasn't militaristic in its force-fulness or authority. The cops tried to move swiftly, but Garth couldn't help acknowledging the fans yelling for him to look their way or touch their outstretched hands. He claims to look forward to these opportunities to connect with his fans one-on-one, even if the individual sessions last an average of thirty seconds each.

"Those people have given me everything," he said the day of the autograph signing. "How can you say no to your providers? For the distances they drive, or [the times they] sit in the rain, I don't see giving of yourself as that much of a payback. You've got to take care of your people in order for them to have faith in you. That's only fair."

Fans started lining up at Garth's specially designed booth when the gates opened at 10 A.M., through he wasn't scheduled to appear there until four in the afternoon. Several hundred people missed his performance because they didn't want to risk giving up their spot in the autograph line.

Normal procedure for an artist at a Fan Fair booth is to sit behind a table, quickly scribble a signature, smile a polite greeting, perhaps lean forward for a fast snapshot, and look for the next person. Garth broke protocol by standing in front of his table and physically greeting each fan with a hug or a handshake.

Bowen, who has never been one to hide his cynicism at the antics of his stars, asserts that Garth is as he presents himself—a truly modest, personable gentleman who hasn't lost his earthiness despite his grand vision and ambition.

"I've been in this business for thirty-six years," Bowen told Tannenbaum. "We're all skeptics. So when I met Garth, I thought, 'He can't be real.'" But after seeing him sit consistently for several hours after concerts and obediently sign autographs, Bowen became a convert. "It's just amazing," he said.

When Garth started, he promised his management he would leave the booth by 6 P.M. A Country Music Television cable channel crew set up in a nearby empty building had been catching soundbites from stars all day. The singer had agreed a few days earlier to show up at 5 P.M. He would be the last interview for the crew, which had been hustling through interviews since 10 A.M. His management passed along word that he would keep his appointment, but they needed to wait until six o'clock. They waited.

At 6:30 P.M., however, Garth was continuing to greet fans. At 6:40 P.M., the police escorted him out to a red Chevy pickup, and Garth drove off into the sunset, cameras and fans chasing after him. Eventually, someone informed the CMT crew that Garth had left the building and sped from the fairgrounds.

The singer's day was not over. Several thousand members of his fan club huddled expectantly at the Nashville Convention Center. He'd slept an average of four hours a night for the last month, and the emotional and physical drain of his big day at Fan Fair added to the toll. Still, despite his exhaustion, he tried to not let on to his fans that he felt anything other than extreme gratitude. "I'm so glad to be here with y'all," he told them from the stage as he performed several hits and previewed a couple of new songs from an upcoming third album, including the tender ballad "What's She Doin' Now." He signed autographs and hugged shoulders, stopping occasionally to rub his eyes and drew a deep breath for sustenance. He fought back yawns and tried to act cheerful without coming across as phony. It was harder than usual, but he wasn't about to complain. His eyes may have been hurting, and his legs may have been aching, but Garth Brooks felt better than he had ever felt in his life.

Chapter
☆ 20 ☆

By August 1991, Capitol knew that *Ropin' the Wind* would be bigger than anyone predicted—bigger, perhaps, than anything anyone at the label had ever experienced. Once a small stepchild label that could hardly muster a million sales from a roster of a dozen artists, Capitol suddenly was preparing to ship out the biggest album country music had ever presented to the world.

Behind the scenes, the action got more than tense; Jimmy Bowen's personality swings were growing broader. One day he would jubilantly praise an employee, then lash out at them the next. Nonetheless, the joint was hopping. Besides Garth, Capitol featured more than thirty acts, at least twenty of whom had little or no chance of getting on radio or selling more than thirty thousand discs, at best. For a small staff, the output was astronomical and nearly impossible to treat with the kind of attention necessary to create decent marketing plans or promotion efforts. No one knew who might be blamed for not tucking in this corner or that.

With Garth, though, the plan was clear: He was the priority. He was the savior of Capitol Nashville office. For the rest of their careers, every executive and every underling within Capitol's brick headquarters on Sixteenth Avenue would get jobs easily and proudly impress peers by pointing out that they had helped make Garth Brooks a star. They were a part of the team, the players who helped win the world championship of country music.

By September the machine was working overtime. The advance orders were unprecedented for a Capitol artist—or, for that matter, for any country artist. "We'll ship right at two million [albums], maybe a little more," Joe Mansfield, Capitol's vice president of sales, told *Billboard* magazine.

Capitol had focused all of its guns on preparing the new album for the market and drawing as much attention to it as possible. The company sent out truckloads of three-and-half-foot-tall color posters and other retail paraphernelia designed to plaster store walls, windows, counters, and bins. The promotion material didn't focus simply on the new album. Instead, it pushed all three albums and a video package featuring Garth's three promotional clips.

On September 12, Garth was a guest star on Bob Hope's "Making New Friends" special on NBC-TV. On September 14, he was featured on cable channel VH-1 in its weekly Saturday afternoon "One to One" show. On September 20 and 21, two Garth Brooks concerts were taped to be edited into a long-form concert video. The concerts took place in Dallas, where Garth had broken records by selling out the eighteen thousand seat Reunion Arena in thirty-seven minutes. When the second show was added, it sold another eighteen thousand tickets in an hour.

Joe Harris, the booking agent who handles Garth's concerts for Buddy Lee Attractions, claimed the singer made more than one million dollars in concert earnings in August alone. The same month, Harris told *Billboard*, he turned down another six million in offers that the artist was too busy to take.

Though other artists have entered the market with a couple of million in sales in one week—from Madonna to Metallica to Michael Jackson—it had never happened to a singer wearing a cowboy hat who phrased his words with an unmistakable Southern drawl. *Entertainment Weekly* anticipated his success with a cover story proclaiming him the "most popular singer in America." The same week, *US* magazine hit the stands with a four-page spread celebrating his achievements and his dedication to his fans.

The week ending September 28, when his record went number one, his previous albums were also entrenched in the ranking of the top fifty albums in the United States. As for the country music charts, Garth held three of the top five positions, the others held down by his old rival Clint Black and the other skyrocketing country comer, Travis Tritt.

Through it all, Garth maintained his blend of outspoken humility. When a *Dallas Morning News* scribe implied that country was finally crossing over into the pop market in large numbers, Garth corrected him. "I don't think we're going anywhere. I think the crowds are coming over to country. Country music's in a great driving seat right now."

Perhaps other singers might dispute the claim that Garth was the nation's most popular singer. Surely Michael Jackson, Bruce Springsteen, and Prince were better known. Even if Jackson and Springsteen weren't selling at an astronomical clip in the third week of September 1991, they surely would once they released their anxiously awaited next albums.

In addition, Mariah Carey, Janet Jackson, and Paula Abdul had sold as many albums as Garth during the same period. So who was most popular? In the end, that didn't matter. The important factor was where they started. The others were pop singers and competed in an element where best-sellers were expected to sell in multiple millions.

Garth Brooks, on the other hand, was a country singer. He put out a new album every year. He spent approximately one hundred thousand dollars recording his discs, not seven-figure sums. He had received scant promotion money compared to the others, and his songs could only be heard on country radio, not on CHR or AOR or AC or any of the alphabet radio formats designating the splintered styles of pop music where the big sellers usually were promoted.

"Is he the most popular singer? Gee, I don't know. It's a great story, though," said Geoff Mayfield, *Billboard* associate director of retail research and the compiler of the *Billboard* album chart.

On the day the album hit the streets, a large van pulled up outside of the Capitol Records headquarters at the corner of Sixteenth and Edgehill avenues in the center of Nashville's famed Music Row area. The driver carried in a dozen roses, then another dozen, then several more. In all, one hundred roses were passed out to employees, with the card signed Garth Brooks. He wanted to thank the Capitol staff for working so hard for him. And, of course, he wanted them to keep up the good fight.

Chapter

☆ 21 ☆

No town and no industry celebrates itself as much as the Nashville music community. For every number one record, which amounts to fifty or so a year, someone throws a party. For every new album, for every major concert tour, for every significant or insignificant award, the invitations go out, the bars are set up, the food spread out, and the doors thrown open. It's a small, close community, and they like to pat each other's back.

It creates a good feeling. Achievement gets recognized, people gather away from the rush of business to trade information and catch up on gossip and personal lives. They see each other face-to-face, without having to negotiate or badger. But, with the nonstop celebrations, it gets difficult to tell what's truly important and what's a relatively minor accomplishment.

On September 24, 1991, though, that question didn't exist. Several signs indicated this was no ordinary gathering: Embankments of television cameras and big huddles of crouching photographers. Top executives from nearly every record company. A crowd of several hundred instead of several dozen. Even Jimmy Bowen was there, and he never attends these kinds of functions.

Capitol Records blanketed the city with invitations to a quickly arranged party to celebrate Garth's landmark debut at the top of the pop charts. The company didn't just invite the people involved and the press. They invited every record company, every publishing company, every musician, every songwriter, every member of every organization.

The event took place at the recently opened headquarters of the Country Music Association. The sleek, attractive, one-story building of brick, glass, and muted colors features a large, horseshoe-shaped convention room. A makeshift stage was set in the center of the back wall; separating it from the guests was a barricade of television cameras and battery-generated lights.

Jimmy Bowen, his cloth motorcycle hat

pulled tight over his forehead, walked on stage, gazed over the crowd through his smoke-tinted glasses, and proclaimed that this was a party for all of the country music community. Behind him, an eight-foot-wide blowup of the top ten positions of the *Billboard* album chart announced the good news: Garth Brooks' album sat at number one, one spot ahead of Metallica's.

"Sure, Garth Brooks is great for Capitol Reocrds—you bet he is," Bowen avowed. "But Garth Brooks is also great for all of Nashville and all of country music."

Bowen looked over at the plaques propped up at the side of the stage. He rattled off the honor roll: number one album, number one and number two country album, number one single, number one music video. "This may never happen again in history," Bowen declared. "No one may ever have this many number ones at the same time in our lifetime."

Bowen then emphasized that the celebration went beyond a single artist scoring higher than any country performer before. He opened a *Billboard* chart and found plenty more to celebrate, he said. He saw the most country artists listed among the top two hundred albums ever.

Bowen read off the names: "I see Travis Tritt at number twenty-seven. I see Ricky Van Shelton at number forty-two, and Alan Jackson, Randy Travis, and Trisha Yearwood." He went on to cite every country artist on the charts, including Clint Black, Reba McEntire, Dolly Parton, Lorrie Morgan, Doug Stone, Diamond Rio, Brooks & Dunn, George Strait, the Judds, the Kentucky HeadHunters, Vince Gill, Mary Chapin-Carpenter, Sawyer Brown, Kathy Mattea, Aaron Tippin, Mark Chesnutt, Pirates of the Mississippi, Keith Whitley, Billy Dean, Alabama, Patty Loveless, and Dwight Yoakam.

He took a deep breath as he ended. "How about that, Nashville? Doesn't sound like a fluke, does it?"

Bowen then introduced Joe Smith, president of Capitol Records's worldwide operation, who had flown in from Los Angeles to attend the celebration. Bowen joked about how often he has worked with Smith over the last three decades. "Everywhere I go, he turns out to be my boss," Bowen quipped.

In 1979, when Smith was president of Elektra Records, he hired Bowen to run the Nashville operation. Then, when Smith took over the reins at Capitol Records in the late 1980s, he persuaded Bowen to leave his position as president of MCA's Nashville division to take a similar post at Capitol/Nashville. Bowen made the move.

"At Elektra, things worked out pretty good," Bowen noted. "But this time it really worked out well, hasn't it, Joe?"

Smith is a short, thick-bodied former radio announcer with a long history in the music business and a reputation as an immaculately fashionable dresser with a ribald wit. He started his speech with a remark about Bowen's lack of sartorial care: The executive was dressed in a casual sports shirt, loose blue denim trousers, a waist-length athletic jacket, and his trademark cloth hat. "I've been working with him for twenty years now, and he hasn't improved his wardrobe a bit, has he? I have no influence with him in that area."

A popular speaker, Smith was the only speaker of the day easily heard above the din of music people, many of whom ignored the proceedings in order to meet, greet, trade stories, order drinks, and generally act merry.

"What a great day this is," Smith started. "What keeps us loving this business and staying in this business is seeing a truly talented artist succeed on this kind of level. It creates an excitement we can all feel. When somebody you hadn't heard of two years ago is sweeping the country and bringing people into record stores because they must have a copy of his music. That's what it's about."

Smith paused, smiling broadly as he gazed at Garth, whose mouth was curled in as if he was biting his lip. "And if you wanted to build a prototype of what a superstar should be, Garth Brooks is it. I have to tell you, it's terrific to be involved with a young man with his character and his kind of solid sense of himself. It's truly unusual."

Smith noted that, beyond the widely publicized sales figures his albums had speedily accumulated, the recently released video compilation of three songs had sold nearly a quarter of a million copies in less than two months. He also mentioned the long-form video shot two days earlier and called it "probably one of the best ever filmed."

Smith then called Garth to the stage. Wearing a black crew-neck sweater and acid-washed blue jeans, he ambled on stage like a self-conscious linebacker surprised with an honor at a sports banquet. He moved slow and with lots of body motion. The surprise was the third platinum record certification, confirming that Ropin' the Wind had topped the three-million-sales plateau.

"You guys gonna have a lot of kids," Smith jibed, " 'cause you're gonna need them to help carry all the awards Garth is gonna win. We're getting a glare burn from all this reflecting glass up here."

Smith then gave the microphone back to Bowen to make the formal introduction of his star. "Garth Brooks has set a new benchmark in this community, and you're going to see him continue to succeed because he's got his head on straight and he's got some very creative ideas on how to reach people," Bowen said. "He's showing you how you do when you earn this kind of success. He's a fine young man."

Garth then moseyed forward, still walking in the same manner that John Wayne used when he lumbered into a bar in a Western movie. After a rousing ovation, he stroked his face and without looking upward, he said, "I've learned a lot of things from Mr. Bowen, and dressing is one of them." Then looking up to gaze the room, he added, "If I knew this was going to be this big a deal, I would have dressed for it."

He then put to rest any question of tension between him and Bowen. "I've read that Mr. Bowen and Mr. Smith have said that they're not sure how to read me sometimes. Well, I hope this is clear. I want them to be sure and let me know if they're ever leaving and going anywhere, 'cause I want my butt right with you wherever you go."

He then paused for several seconds, pausing

dramatically to take a deep breath. "This has been quite a week, and I don't know if this guy deserves it," he said. "I just think country music is finally getting what it deserves. It's the number one form of music on this planet."

The same day, NBC announced that Garth Brooks would host his first television special in the fall. "There is rarely a performer who explodes with the popularity that Garth Brooks has," said Rick Ludwin, senior vice president of specials for NBC. "We're tremendously pleased that his first TV special will be with us at NBC."

Chapter

☆ **22** ☆

By October 2, 1991, heaping more awards on Garth Brooks seemed anticlimactic. Less than a month earlier, he had set precedents unthinkable for country music artists in previous years or decades.

The CMA gives out an Entertainer of the Year award every year, and 1991 was Garth's first nomination. He and his songs also were among the five nominees each for Best Album, Best Song, Best Single, and Best Male Vocalist.

No matter who won what, no one in country music had accomplished more in such a short time. Before the show he said he would walk out of the building happy, whatever the outcome. He'd spent the week at home, a rare luxury. His parents had been staying at his home for an extended vacation, an even rarer treat.

Still, a certain tension goes with any awards ceremony. Garth, ever blunt, told anyone who asked that, sure he would like to win. Deep down, he's a competitor first and foremost.

The tension eased early. "Friends in Low Places" was named Best Single in the first award of the night. Not long afterward, *No Fences* took Best Album of the Year. Later in the program "The Thunder Rolls" slapped back at country's cable channels by becoming Video of the Year.

Garth still found a way to pump excitement into a night that belonged to him. In a daringly dynamic performance, the singer ripped into a stunning, archly dramatic version of "Shameless," a Billy Joel song featured on Garth's *Ropin' the Wind* album. It takes more than talent to connect so deeply with a song; it takes a whole lot of soul and an ultimately life-affirming belief that communication, conviction, and honesty matter.

When accepting country music's most prestigious annual honor, the CMA Entertainer of the Year Award, Garth stood on stage and stared at the trophy. Then, as he spoke, he used the point of the glass obelisk to scratch the side of his head.

"This is cool," he said softly. "It's funny how a chubby kid can just be having fun and they call it entertaining." He then paid tribute to the singers he often refers to as his heroes, the "Georges"—country stars George Strait and George Jones, both of whom were in the audience.

He then remembered another well-known George was in the audience. "No offense, Mr. President," he said with an engaging smile, gesturing toward George Bush, who sat with his wife Barbara in the second row of the Grand Ole Opry House.

Backstage, music industry veterans were already assessing the future of the first country singer to earn the description of America's favorite singer. "I think too much can be bad for Garth Brooks," said Ken Kragen, a veteran artist manager who has worked with Kenny Rogers for more than two decades. "He's enough of a sharp guy to realize that this year's sweep is next year's shutout."

Garth took a similar line, since humility is always the best tact when victory has been expected. In one year he went from winning the CMA's version of a best new artist award to becoming the dominant force in the genre and deservingly winning the Entertainer of the Year

Award through the votes of his peers and associates.

He was the first artist in history to leap from the new artist award to the top entertainer. He didn't point that out. Instead, he noted that he could slip back down the ladder just as quickly as he had climbed it.

Less than six years earlier he had stood on a balcony of a hotel, letting the rain wash across his face but not letting it ease the pain of rejection he felt. As the rain washed over him, he thought about how hard he had worked to gain recognition as an athlete, as a student, as a friend, as a family member.

Garth Brooks had always wondered if he had what it takes to truly excel and to be recognized for it. No matter what happens in the future, in the fall of 1991, he stood upon a plateau no country music entertainer had ever reached.

DISCOGRAPHY FOR
GARTH BROOKS

(All Albums Recorded at Jack's Tracks Recording
Studio, Nashville, Tennessee)

GARTH BROOKS (1989)
Produced by Allen Reynolds
Recorded and Mixed by Mark Miller
Mastered by Denny Purcell at Georgetown Masters

Not Counting You
(Garth Brooks)

I've Got a Good Thing Going
(Larry Bastian/Mahl/Garth Brooks)

If Tomorrow Never Comes
(Kent Blazy/Garth Brooks)

Everytime That It Rains
(Charley Stefl/England/Garth Brooks)

Alabama Clay
(Larry Cordle/R. Scaife)

Much Too Young (To Feel This Damn Old)
(R. Taylor/Garth Brooks)

Cowboy Bill
(Larry Bastian/E. Berghoff)

Nobody Gets Off in This Town
(Larry Bastian/Dewayne Blackwell)

I Know One
(Jack Clement)

The Dance
(Tony Arata)

HARMONY VOCALS: Garth Brooks, Alabama Clay; Wayland Patton, Kathy Chlavola, "If Tomorrow Never Comes"; Hurshel Wiginton, Jennifer O'Brien, Wendy Johnson, and Curtis Young; "Everytime That It Rains," "I've Got a Good Thing Going."
DRUMS: Milton Sledge
BASS: Mike Chapman
ELECTRIC GUITARS: Chris Leuzinger
ACOUSTIC GUITARS: Mark Casstevens
KEYBOARDS: Bobby Wood
STEEL GUITAR: Bruce Bouton
FIDDLE: Rob Hajacos
STRINGS: The Nashville String Machine: Carl Gorodetzky, Dennis Molchan, Pamela Sixfin, John Borg, George Binkley III, Roy Christensen, and Gary Vanosdale
STRING ARRANGEMENTS: Charles Cochran

NO FENCES (1990)
Produced by Allen Reynolds
Recorded and Mixed by Mark Miller
Mastered by Denny Purcell at Georgetown Masters

The Thunder Rolls
(Pat Alger/Garth Brooks)

New Way to Fly
(Kim Williams/Garth Brooks)

Two of a Kind, Workin' On a Full House
(Bobby Boyd/Warren Dale Haynes/Dennis Robbins)

Victim of the Game
(Mark D. Sanders/Garth Brooks)

Friends in Low Places
(Dewayne Blackwell/Bud Lee)

Wild Horses
(Bill Shore/David Wills)

Unanswered Prayers
(Pat Alger/Larry B. Bastian/Garth Brooks)

Same Old Story
(Tony Arata)

Mr. Blue
(Dewayne Blackwell)

Wolves
(Stephanie Davis)

HARMONY VOICES: Garth Brooks, Trish Yearwood, Wendy Johnson, Jennifer O'Brien, Hurshel Wiginton, Curtis Young

VOCAL GROUP ON "FRIENDS IN LOW PLACES": Pat Alger, Al "Shaggy" Barclay, Dewayne Blackwell, Bruce Bouton, Tim Bowers, Sandy Brooks (the Mrs.), Stephanie C. Brown, Mike Chapman, Bob Doyle, the Englands (plus one), Dave Gant, Rob Hajacos, Joe Harris, Dan Heins, Rusty "Race Horse" Jones, Steve King, Earl of Bud Lee, Pam "The Chick" Lewis, Buddy Mondlock, Steve Morley, Mike "Palmerman," Brian Petree, Dale Pierce, Jim Rooney, Tami Rose, Lee Sartin, Charley Stefl, Scott Stern, Bobby Wood

VOCAL GROUP ON "UNANSWERED PRAYERS": Wendy Johnson, Jennifer O'Brien, Hurshel Wiginton, Curtis Young

VOCAL GROUP ON "WOLVES": Indian River—David McVay, Stephen Tolman, Neil Thrasher, Curry Worsham

BAND AND CREW OF "STILLWATER"
Tim Bowers—Bass Guitar, Vocals
Dave Gant—Keyboards, Fiddles, Vocals
James Garver—Guitars, Fiddles, Vocals
Steve McClure—Steel and Electric Guitars
Ty England—Acoustic Guitars, Vocals
Mike Palmer—Drums, Percussion
Dan Hines—Sound
Brian Petree—Stage Manager
Al "Shaggy" Barclay—Bus Driver
Kelly Brooks—Money Man

MUSICIANS:
ACOUSTIC GUITARS: Pat Alger, Johnny Christopher, Mark Casstevens, Chris Leuzinger
BASS: Mike Chapman, Milton Sledge
DRUMS: Milton Sledge
ELECTRIC GUITAR: Chris Leuzinger
ELECTRIC PIANO, PIANO AND KEYBOARDS: Bobby Wood
STEEL GUITAR: Bruce Bouton
FIDDLE: Rob Hajacos
UPRIGHT STRING BASS: Edgar Meyer
STRINGS: Nashville String Machine: George Binkley III, John Borg, Carl Gorodetzky, Lee Larrison, Dennis Molchan, Pamela Sixfin, Mark Tanner, Gary Vanosdale, Kristin Wilkinson
STRING ARRANGEMENT: Charles Cochran

ROPIN' THE WIND (1991)

Produced by Allen Reynolds
Recorded and Mixed by Mark Miller
Mastered by Denny Purcell at Georgetown Masters

Against the Grain

(Bruce Bouton/Larry Cordle/Carl Jackson)

Rodeo

(Larry Bastian)

What She's Doing Now

(Pat Alger/Garth Brooks)

Burning Bridges

(Stephanie C. Brown/Garth Brooks)

Papa Loved Mama
(Kim Williams/Garth Brooks)

Shameless
(Billy Joel)

Cold Shoulder
(Kent Blazy/Kim Williams/Garth Brooks)

We Bury the Hatchet
(Wade Kimes/Garth Brooks)

In Lonesome Dove
(Cynthia Limbaugh/Garth Brooks)

The River
(Victoria Shaw, Garth Brooks)

MUSICIANS
BASS: Mike Chapman
DRUMS, PERCUSSION: Milton Sledge
PERCUSSION: Kenny Malone
KEYBOARDS: Bobby Wood
ELECTRIC GUITARS: Chris Leuzinger
ACOUSTIC GUITARS: Mark Casstevens
FIDDLE: Rob Hajacos
STEEL GUITAR, LAP STEEL, DOBRO: Bruce Bouton
MANDOLIN: Sam Bush
DOBRO: Jerry Douglas
ACOUSTIC BASS: Edgar Meyer
HARMONY VOCALS: Trisha Yearwood, Carl Jackson, Larry
    Cordle, Garth Brooks
STRINGS: The Nashville String Machine: George Bink-

ley III, Roy Christensen, Conni Elisor, Carl Goro-
detzky, Richard Grosjean, Anthony LaMarchina,
Lee Larrison, Theodore Madsen, Dennis Molchan,
Pamela Sixfin, Gary Vanosdale, Kristin Wilkinson
STRING ARRANGEMENTS: Charles Cochran

BAND AND CREW OF "STILLWATER"
Dave Gant—Keyboards, Fiddle, Vocals
Brent Dannen—Stage Sound
Steve McClure—Steel, Electric Guitars
Gaylon Moore—Bus Driver
Kelly Brooks—Money Man
Mike Palmer—Drums, Percussion
Jim Payne—Bus Driver
Brian Petree—Stage Manager
Ty England—Acoustic Guitars, Vocals
Steve Southerland—Bus Driver
Mick Weber—Road Manager
Dave Butzler—Lighting Director
Betsy Smittle—Bass Guitar, Vocals
Mark Greenwood—Stage Manager
Dan Heins—House Sound
James Garver—Electric Guitars, Percussion, Vocals
John McBride—Production Manager

ABOUT THE AUTHOR

MICHAEL MCCALL is a freelance journalist specializing in popular music and the entertainment industry. He was a staff writer for seven years for the *Nashville Banner* focusing on music, and currently writes a column for the *Nashville Scene,* an independent weekly. Additional stories by Michael McCall have appeared in *US, Billboard,* the *Christian Science Monitor,* the *San Francisco Examiner, Country America, Southern Magazine,* and a wide range of specialized music magazines. He lives in Nashville.

Visit the
Simon & Schuster Web site:
www.SimonSays.com

and sign up for our
mystery e-mail updates!

Keep up on the latest
new releases, author appearances,
news, chats, special offers, and more!
We'll deliver the information
right to your inbox — if it's new,
you'll know about it.

SIMON & SCHUSTER
A VIACOM COMPANY
www.SimonSays.com

POCKET BOOKS   POCKET STAR BOOKS